HAVE YOU EVER...?

Have you ever found it difficult to teach the Faith? Have your friends ever gotten angry with you because you refuse to backbite? Do you ever find it difficult to get along with others, even though you know, as a Bahá'í, you should love everyone? Have you ever felt just a little bit neglected because your parents have so many Bahá'í activities? Have you ever felt just a little 'different' and alone because you try to be a good Bahá'í and your non-Bahá'í friends don't understand?

Well, cheer up, because thousands of Bahá'í young people the world over have, at one time or another, felt just as you do. The fact is, feeling 'different' is just what being a Bahá'í is all about. We are among the first Bahá'ís to try and put the wonderful teachings of Bahá'u'lláh into practice, and everybody knows it's not easy to be the first to do something new.

In this book you will meet Lucy, Ralph, Carrie, Nick and many other young people who, just like you, are trying to understand what being a Bahá'í is all about. So, sit back and enjoy it – and who knows? You might find someone just like you!

This book is dedicated to Andishey Hanbury, and to all teenage pioneers in Africa. May the Blessed Beauty watch over them, inspire their hearts and grant them perseverance in their heroic sacrifices – sacrifices of a kind that perhaps often go unrecognized.

A for Effort

And Other Stories for Today's Young Heroes

by

Susan J. Allen

ONEWORLD

OXFORD

A for Effort
And Other Stories for Today's Young Heroes

Oneworld Publications Ltd
(Sales and Editorial)
185 Banbury Road, Oxford, OX2 7AR, England

Oneworld Publications Ltd
(U.S. Sales Office)
County Route 9, P.O. Box 357
Chatham, N.Y. 12037, USA

© Susan J. Allen 1992
All rights reserved. Copyright under Berne Convention
'The Shawl and the Book' was first published in
Brilliant Star (September/October 1985).

A CIP record for this book is available from the British Library

ISBN 1-85168-034-9

Phototypeset by Intype, London
Printed and bound in Great Britain
by The Guernsey Press

CONTENTS

A For Effort 1
That Tingly Feeling 9
Lucy's Magic Promise 21
What's a Little Sweeping? 31
The Shawl and the Book 41
African Blues 47
A Time for Everything 61
Play it Right 71
Beyond All That 83
Four Simple Words 95
Sunday's Fire 103
Piece of Cake 109
Some Summer 119

A FOR EFFORT

Lisa, Jessica and Anita stood on the school playground, the cold autumn wind whipping through their hair. Jessica was watching a group of girls across the schoolyard.

"Just look at her," she murmured spitefully.

"Look at who?" asked Lisa, wrapping her jacket more closely around her.

"Why Janet, that new girl. She thinks she's so wonderful."

"Yeah," Anita joined in gleefully.

Lisa felt uncomfortable. She always felt uncomfortable when her friends started backbiting. Lisa was a Bahá'í and knew it was wrong. She knew she shouldn't even listen – but then she never knew what to say when it happened. She frowned, her pixie face crinkling up trying to think of an answer. Finally she said, "Oh Jessica, Janet's not that bad. What did she ever do to you?"

"Why, she thinks she's better than me. She won't even talk to me. And her clothes, always *so* frilly . . . like she was some kind of princess." She looked down with approval at her own stonewashed jeans.

"I think she always looks nice," said Lisa. "She probably doesn't talk to you because she's new here and doesn't know you. She's not even in your class. I think she's shy. Anyway, have you even met her yet?"

"I don't need to. I can tell I don't like her just by the way she walks!"

"Jessica, that's silly."

"Whose friend are you, anyway?" Jessica snapped. "You're always taking everybody else's side. Sometimes I don't think you're my friend at all!" At that she turned on her heel and stalked off.

"Yeah!" said Anita as a parting shot and followed her friend.

Lisa stood alone on the playground, her hands balled into tight fists in her pockets. *What's the use?* she thought with despair. Sometimes being a Bahá'í made her feel so alone. Only yesterday she'd lost another friend. Mary had forgotten her homework and wanted to copy Lisa's. Lisa had refused as gently as she could. She tried to explain that it wasn't honest, but Mary hadn't understood. She thought Lisa was just being selfish.

After school that afternoon, Lisa tossed her books on the living room couch and flopped down beside them, not even bothering to take off her jacket. Her older brother Gary stood by the kitchen door. He raised an eyebrow. "Tough day, kid?" He smiled playfully.

Lisa looked up at her brother and was struck by how different they were. At nineteen he was tall, dark and good-looking. Somehow, looking at him always made her feel glad. But today she didn't smile back. She looked down and sighed, nervously fingering the buttons of her jacket.

Gary slid down beside her. "So, what's up?"

Lisa didn't say anything for a moment. She brushed her blond curls from her face and sighed again. "Gary," she said suddenly, "what do *you* say when people backbite?"

"Oh, so that's it. Trouble with friends?"

"Yeah."

"Well, that *is* a tough question. Sometimes I try to change the subject . . . and sometimes I try to say something nice about that person."

"I tried that and lost two friends."

"So maybe they're not real friends."

Lisa studied Gary. He always seemed so happy and carefree. Mom and Dad were proud of him. He was the most active Bahá'í youth in the community and was always the first to take part in teaching projects. Lisa adored him and thought how nice it would be to be so charming and easy with people. With Gary, it was just second nature.

"But Gary," she said, "Jessica's not that bad — sometimes she's quite nice. Anyway, if I stayed away from everyone who backbites, I wouldn't have *any* friends at school . . . Sometimes I feel so different from the other kids."

"Well, of course you're different, Lisa." Gary laughed. "You're a Bahá'í. If you were like everyone else what would be the use of being a Bahá'í? It's by being different that you teach everyone how wonderful being a Bahá'í is." He paused. "You know that's how 'Abdu'l-Bahá taught, don't you?"

Lisa thought of the stories about 'Abdu'l-Bahá that she'd heard all her life. She nodded slowly.

"He was *always* good, noble and completely honest. It must have been difficult for Him when so many people around Him were not honest and were even sometimes plotting against him."

"I know," murmured Lisa. And she did. Hadn't she

A for Effort

been trying to follow 'Abdu'l-Bahá's example? Isn't that how she lost her friends?

"Why don't you just tell me what happened today?"

Lisa poured out the whole story, including the earlier incident with Mary.

Gary, his forehead creased in thoughtfulness, sat for a moment. Then he said, "It seems like the only thing to do is try to continue being like 'Abdu'l-Bahá. I mean, show so much love and consideration to these girls that they can't fail to see that you mean well."

"But they probably won't even speak to me!"

"I didn't say they'd notice right away. Sometimes these things take time. You remember the story of 'Abdu'l-Bahá and the man who hated Him for twenty-four years, don't you?"

Lisa nodded. It was their Dad's favorite story.

"Well, that man showed hate to 'Abdu'l-Bahá for all those years and 'Abdu'l-Bahá showed him only love and kindness, bringing him food when he was hungry and even a doctor when he was sick . . . and finally he came to 'Abdu'l-Bahá's door and asked to be forgiven."

"But these girls aren't hungry and they don't need a doctor!"

"Sure, but everyone needs love. Of course, you'll have to be sincere. You'll have to really love them and to do that you'll have to look at their good points . . . and forget the bad."

Good points, thought Lisa. Well, she guessed she could find some. She could try.

"I can try."

"Look kid," he smiled, "you've already been trying. Do you think you'd be having these problems if you weren't? That's the whole point. Being a good Bahá'í, changing yourself to be like 'Abdu'l-Bahá, means one test after another. But," he added, "how do you feel after you've passed a really difficult test with an A+?"

"Great!"

"Okay, so try for that A+." Gary got up. He looked down at her. "And take that coat off, will you? It makes me hot just looking at you!"

During the next few days Lisa tried to greet both Jessica and Anita as if nothing had happened. They would answer her but then move off. Lisa was hurt, but she *tried* to think of their good points and not be angry. She knew Jessica was good at math – maybe she could ask for help with her homework. Anita would be playing in a piano recital soon. She decided to go.

She did see Janet who had just moved in a few houses away from her.

"Your friends, Jessica and Anita," Janet asked one day, "you said they were your friends. What are they like?"

Lisa was still feeling hurt, but she didn't let on. She talked about Jessica and Anita as if they were still her friends and tried to think of nice things to say about them.

Then one day, Lisa found herself behind Jessica and Anita in the school cafeteria lunch line. Jessica was frantically searching through her purse. "Oh no, I left my lunch money at home!" she wailed.

Lisa thought for a moment and then made up her mind. She stepped forward and said timidly, "I'm not hungry today, Jessica. I was just going to buy some milk. If you want, I can lend you my lunch money."

A for Effort

Jessica looked at her in surprise. "Well, if you're really not hungry..."

"I... I'm not," she said and pressed the money into Jessica's hand. Jessica accepted it with a shy smile.

"Thanks," she said.

After being served Lisa, Jessica and Anita sat together at a cafeteria table. Lisa had her carton of milk in front of her and tried not to notice the rumblings in her stomach, while Jessica gobbled down her lunch. Lisa was confused. She was glad to be able to be like 'Abdu'l-Bahá in some small way. After all, Jessica was hungry and Lisa fed her. Still, she couldn't quite get over her hurt feelings.

"This *is* good, want some?" offered Jessica.

Lisa noticed that there wasn't much left. "That's okay, I'm not hungry."

At that moment Janet came up and set her tray down next to Lisa. Jessica smirked and jabbed Anita in the ribs with her elbow.

"Hi!" said Janet cheerfully.

"Hi," said Lisa, making room for her. Not knowing what else to do, she added, "These are my friends..."

"Jessica and Anita." Janet finished. "I know, you told me all about them." She smiled at the two girls.

Jessica, her eyes narrowed, asked sharply, "Is that so? What did she say?"

"Let's see, you're good at math and Anita, she plays the piano. She's playing in a recital Friday night. And... you're both her good friends."

Jessica looked unsure of herself. "That's *all* she said?"

Janet looked bewildered. "I don't remember anything else."

"I mean," Janet continued, "she didn't just say good

things. She must have said *something* else." Jessica couldn't believe Lisa hadn't said anything about their spat.

Janet just looked puzzled. "You mean like something bad?"

"Yeah, like something bad."

"*Lisa?*" asked Janet in surprise. Then she laughed. "Why, I've never heard Lisa say anything bad about anyone." She patted Lisa's hand. "I don't think she knows how."

For a moment, Jessica sat there studying Lisa's lowered head and the empty carton of milk in front of her. Slowly, a spark of understanding lit up in Jessica's eyes. She turned to Janet and in amazed tones said, "You know, I think you're right!"

That afternoon after school, Lisa dashed up the porch steps at home and burst in the front door. Gary looked up in surprise from where he sat reading, took one look at Lisa's flushed face and said happily, "Back to normal, I see."

"Yeah," she answered, setting her books down and hanging up her coat.

"A+?"

Lisa paused and frowned ever so slightly. "Well, maybe a B."

"So, sit down and tell me about it."

When she was finished talking he asked, "So, why a B?"

"Well," she said slowly, "before Janet came to the table I was still a little angry. I mean, I gave Jessica my lunch and everything, but . . . I just didn't feel like maybe 'Abdu'l-Bahá would . . ."

Gary reached over and ruffled her unruly curls.

"Next time, kid. But now we'll just call it A for Effort."

Lisa looked up into her brother's face and grinned. "Okay," she said, "until next time."

THAT TINGLY FEELING

So there I was, wondering what it would be like to be a super space hero and to die bravely on a strange new planet and be famous and everything, when I suddenly got an awful thought. I mean, like what if I died on another planet? Maybe I'd never see Bahá'u'lláh. I mean, maybe on another planet they'd have *different* Prophets – green with six eyes or something. Now I *know* the Spirit would be the same, same light different lamp and all that, but I did so want to see Bahá'u'lláh Himself some day. That was why I was being mega good (well, from time to time) teaching, giving half my allowance to the Arc Fund, smiling lovingly at my dear sweet little sister when I'd really like to brain her . . . That wasn't the *only* reason, of course, (that I was being good). A little while back it sort of came to me that things just *worked* better when I was good. I mean, Dad wouldn't have to glare at me and grit his teeth (instead of shouting) when he tried so hard to be patient. And Mom, Mom would look at me with misty eyes and a damp smile every time my $1.50 clinked inside the special 'Arc Box' (that I'd made from nifty space shuttle wrapping paper and cardboard) and say, "You're a good boy, Ralph." It may not sound like much (those five little words) but it always made me feel kind of tingly inside and somehow I'd know that when she said that, Bahá'u'lláh (or 'Abdu'l-Bahá too, for that matter) was up there smiling at me.

Anyway, (where was I? Oh yeah – space hero) I decided maybe I *wouldn't* be a space hero, maybe I'd be a fireman instead, except that that was what I wanted to be when I was five and I was getting a little old for that now. So maybe I'd be a pilot. That was close enough to home that ... But I didn't get any further because the spiritual portion of the Feast ended. I knew it because the secretary said, "And now, the spiritual part of the Feast has ended."

"Oh no!" I groaned inwardly. I'd done it again. Daydreaming in Feast. I mean, I really *tried* to pay attention, I could even tell you which first two prayers were said. I admit, after that things got a little fuzzy. I guiltily glanced over at Mom, sure that she'd noticed. But she just smiled that "You're a good boy" smile and that made me feel worse. Andy was motioning me to go downstairs (we're allowed to go downstairs after the devotional part of the Feast) but (I don't know why) I shook my head. I guess I thought I should do a few minutes penance for daydreaming in Feast. Anyway, that's when I heard the suggestion. "We should find creative new ways to teach the Faith." I can't say I really heard much more after that. Guess I was daydreaming again, and then I came to my senses and went downstairs to play with Andy. But that sentence somehow stuck in my mind.

"What's a creative way to teach?" I asked Mom on the way home.

"Oh, I guess it means to find new, different, interesting ways to teach."

Hmmm ... I thought. That's kind of up my alley. I mean, I *like* interesting things.

"Maybe like teaching different extra-terrestrial beings or something... *That* would be interesting." I said hopefully.

Mom giggled. At *her* age, she still giggled. A girl's a girl, I thought. "I don't think that's what he had in mind, Ralph," she said.

"They probably have their own Prophets anyway."

"What, honey?"

"Oh, never mind."

The next few days I was busy – thinking. A creative way to teach... It's easier than it sounds, believe me. Not that I didn't have lots of ideas – like scattering pamphlets in the shape of space shuttles (to make them more 'creative') out of an airplane (that I would pilot myself) or renting a blimp that trailed a banner reading "BAHÁ'U'LLÁH HAS COME" with my name and address in big letters at the end of it. Somehow, none of those ideas seemed to be within my means.

Finally, one morning, while watching Mom shuffle around the kitchen in her Micky Mouse slippers (she'll *never* grow up) I hit on it.

I made my plans.

The next day after dinner, while Mom was washing and Dad drying, I made my requests.

"Twenty cups of flour," I announced.

Mom turned around. "What?"

"I need twenty cups of flour."

"Whatever for?" she asked, shooting Dad one of her desperate 'What's he got up his sleeve now?' looks.

"Well," I said, pulling out a crumpled sheet of paper with a recipe I had laboriously copied, "it says here two cups of flour and I figure I'll need ten times that. I've got it all figured out."

A for Effort

"You've got *what* figured out?"

"All the things I need for my creative teaching project."

"*What* creative teaching project is this?"

"The one I'm doing Saturday afternoon."

"Oh, *that* teaching project," said Dad folding up the dish towel (I think he was glad for the excuse). "Why don't you tell us about it?"

"When the dishes are washed," Mom said firmly.

Dad unfolded his towel.

After the dishes were washed and neatly put away and the towel refolded, we sat down at the kitchen table.

I brought out my list again. "Let's see, twenty cups of flour, five cups of white sugar, five cups of brown sugar..."

"Ralph," Dad interrupted, "why don't you tell us about it first."

I shifted uneasily in my seat. "Well, actually... it's a bit of a surprise."

"Ralph," Dad said, "you can't expect us to go along without knowing..." Mom put her hand lightly on Dad's shoulder giving her loving, 'Now let's be patient, dear,' look.

"Okay," she said, "what do you need? If it sounds reasonable, Dad and I will consult about it.

I gave them the basic chocolate chip recipe multiplied ten times and then added, "Red M & Ms, butterscotch chips, white chewing gum, twenty copies of the Peace Message, twenty pamphlets (with more ready in the house just in case) and," I looked at Mom, "you."

"Why me?"

"*You* need to help me make the cookies."

"Oh. And why red M & Ms and... chewing gum?"

"I need something brown, red, yellow and white.

"Maybe coconut would do better for the white," Mom suggested diplomatically.

"That's a great idea, Mom. And I also need a small table, two chairs, a big board and brown, red, yellow and white poster paint . . . and a paint brush."

There was a moment of silence and then Dad gave Mom his 'Let's go consult,' look and Mom said, "We'll be back in a moment, dear."

I waited patiently. Mom and Dad often consulted about things since they had become Bahá'ís the year before. They were getting better at it. It had been a long time since *anybody* had yelled in the house (except me and my baby sister, that is, and *I* was getting better too).

Mom and Dad had neglected to close the kitchen door and try as I might not to listen, the words just kind of drifted in.

"What *could* he be planning?" asked Mom.

"I don't know. Knowing Ralph it could be anything, but I hate to discourage him in teaching the Faith. I mean, what could be more important for him to learn?"

"You're right," Mom said. "We always tell him how important it is to teach, now I guess we'll have to show our support."

Pause.

"But what if it's something *really* far out? You don't think he could hurt the Faith, do you?"

Another pause.

"No, I don't think so, and we could always step in at the last moment. Let's try to have a little confidence in him."

Mom and Dad came back into the kitchen. "Okay Ralph, we're behind you."

"Great!" I cried, trying to sound surprised.

"Only one thing," Dad added as a second thought. "You're not going to do anything big, are you? Like teaching in a shopping center. Because in that case we'd have to consult the LSA."

"I won't leave the front yard."

"Okay then, go to it."

The next day was Friday and after school I set to work. I had enlisted Andy's help, so he came over. Frankly he was a bit doubtful about the whole thing. He said he'd never taught the Faith before. I told him that in that case it was a good time to learn. Why, all kinds of people were just waiting to hear about Bahá'u'lláh and who was going to tell them if we didn't? And just for good measure I added, "And Andy, once we tell all the people on earth, then we can go out in space and teach the whole universe!"

Andy did get enthused about that. In fact, he wanted to start designing the space ship right away. But I pointed out that we hadn't done our job on earth yet. I didn't mention that all those aliens probably had their own Prophets – after all, I didn't *know* that, did I?

We emerged from the garage two hours later, splattered with red, brown, yellow and white paint. We had finished our sign. I told Dad that maybe he could leave the car in the driveway that night because we didn't want anyone looking at our 'surprise'. Dad ran his fingers through his hair twice and then finally managed a tight smile. "Whatever you say, Ralph."

The big day came. Mom, Andy and I spent the morning making cookies with my little sister 'helping' (she ate the yellow, brown and green M & Ms that we didn't use). The cookies were a masterpiece.

Each cookie was covered with brown chocolate chips, red M & Ms, yellow butterscotch chips and white coconut.

Mom and Dad looked a little unsure as I popped them into the oven. "Don't you think it's a bit much – all those different things?' asked Mom.

But I reassured them. "Just think of all the different things you get. Why, you'd have to buy five different kinds of cookies to get all that. This way you get them all in one bite!"

Dad still looked a little queasy – but then he's like that. He doesn't even mix his potatoes and peas.

Three o'clock rolled around and Andy and I got ready. We put the table in the front yard near the sidewalk and put two chairs behind it. We piled all the cookies on the table and set out the pamphlets and Peace Messages in a big sack on the ground next to the chairs. Then we proudly brought out our sign. It read: BAHÁ'Í COOKIES 10¢ a piece (cheaper by the dozen) REPRESENTING THE FOUR COLORS OF THE FAMILY OF MAN. It was decorated with pictures of people of different races.

Mom and Dad were sure surprised and I was excited when someone stopped right away. A man got out of his car and walked up to the table.

"What have we here?" he asked.

"They're Bahá'í cookies," I announced proudly. I then waited expectantly for the question which I was sure would follow. "What's Bahá'í?" or at least, "What are Bahá'í cookies?"

Instead he said curtly, "I'll take six."

I was a little taken aback but obediently put the six cookies in a brown paper bag and accepted his change. He left.

A for Effort

I sat down again, trying not to look at Mom and Dad who were trying not to look at me.

Dad cleared his throat. "Hmmm ... Son, I think you forgot something."

"What?" I asked, inspecting the table, "Oh yeah, my change box."

"No."

"What then?"

"I think you forgot to pray."

"Rats!" I cried, slapping the side of my head. "I forgot all about it!"

"It's not too late," said Dad, slipping a prayer book from his shirt pocket with a smile.

Mom and Dad brought lawn chairs for themselves and my little sister and we managed to say three teaching prayers before the next customer arrived.

It was an old man who came up on foot. I shut my prayer book quickly. I was ready.

"Bahá'í cookies, huh?"

"Yes, sir."

"So, what's Bahá'í?"

"It's a religion."

"Yes ... ?"

I panicked — suddenly all the answers I had prepared went out of my head. "And these are Bahá'í cookies." Of all the dumb things to say!

He looked puzzled. I can't say that I blamed him.

"So the people in your religion make cookies?"

"No sir, I mean ... yes sir. I mean *I'm* a Bahá'í and *I* made the cookies but other Bahá'ís don't."

He looked more puzzled.

I took a deep breath. "What I mean is, I call these Bahá'í cookies because ... I mean, if you just look at the cookies, they have all different colors on them, see?" I picked up a cookie. "Brown, red, yellow and white. These are the colors of the different people of the world..."

I took another deep breath. "So, I put all the colors of the people of the world on one cookie just to show that all the people of the world should live together in peace and..."

"And eat the same cookies," he finished.

"Yes, sir, no, I mean no sir... I mean..." I looked at him and noticed that he was chuckling. I blushed.

"I know what you mean, son. You want to say that your religion believes that all the people should live together peacefully."

I sighed, "Yes, sir."

"Well, I think that's just fine, I'll take a dozen."

I counted out a dozen and handed them to him. Just as he was about to leave Andy gave me a small kick in the shin. He pointed to the bag at my feet.

"Oh, sir," I said, taking a Peace Message and a pamphlet out of the bag, "if you're interested in the Bahá'í Faith I can give you something to read..."

He paused. "I think I'd like that," he answered.

Before he left two more people came up and then some neighborhood kids and then more people and to make a long story short, we gave away exactly seventeen Peace Messages and pamphlets and sold 182 cookies (my little sister having eaten nine).

By the end of the day, my voice was hoarse from talking. Unfortunately, I had to spend so much time explaining what the Bahá'í Faith had to do with cookies and worse still, how a *cookie* could be Bahá'í that I decided maybe next time I found a creative way to teach, I'd leave cookies out of it. Still, I did get to tell lots of people about the Faith and Mom and Dad and even Andy did some talking too.

Andy and I counted up our money at the end of the

day. "Why, that's just enough for that new model space station I saw at the store the other day," exclaimed Andy.

I thought about that. "No Andy. I don't think so."

"Well, then we could save it to build our own space ship – you know, for after the world becomes Bahá'í and everything."

"Andy, we only told seventeen people about the Faith. There are still a couple billion left to go."

Andy looked distressed. "Well, how many cookies do we have to make anyway?"

"Andy, we don't have to make cookies for everyone we teach! Besides, we're not the only ones teaching. I mean, there's the LSA and everything.

"But," I said, getting back to the subject at hand, "when it comes to using the money to teach, the best way is just to give it to the Arc."

"The Arc?"

"You know, the buildings they're putting up near the Shrine of the Báb. Remember what they said in children's class?"

"Oh yeah, those." Andy sounded doubtful.

"Well, Mom says they don't have enough money yet and that's because Bahá'ís aren't giving enough. She says that if everyone gave, there'd be plenty of money."

"So, how's that going to teach the Faith?"

"Well," I said, not too sure of myself, "people will look at those buildings and say: 'Hey, what's that?' and someone will say. 'Bahá'í buildings,' and they'll ask, 'What's Bahá'í?' just like people said, 'What are Bahá'í cookies?' and then someone will give them a Peace Message and a pamphlet and they'll become Bahá'ís."

"No one became a Bahá'í today, Ralph."

"They just gotta think about it first. Anyway, I think they're going to use those buildings too – for libraries and stuff.

"Anyway, we gotta give this money because the Universal House of Justice says we should and Mom says that whenever the Universal House of Justice says to do something it's just like Bahá'u'lláh said it. So, we gotta do it."

"Oh," said Andy, "in *that* case, okay."

Andy and I went in the house and took down my nifty space shuttle Arc Fund box. We put in the money, dollar by dollar and coin by coin.

Just as the last coin dropped in with a clink, I noticed Mom and Dad standing behind us. Dad had his arm around Mom and they were both smiling. Mom's eyes were all misty and (just like I told you) she said, "You're a good boy, Ralph." There it was, that tingly feeling again, and somehow I knew that Bahá'u'lláh (*and* 'Abdu'l-Bahá for that matter) was up there somewhere smiling at me too.

LUCY'S MAGIC PROMISE

"Oh drat!" said Lucy, pulling at the thin black cane.

"What's the matter?" called her mother from the kitchen. Mrs. Busby appeared at the dining room door.

"I can't get this cane to work! What *am* I going to do? Holly's party is Friday and I need it for the magic show!" Lucy slumped against the wall and inspected the cane more closely. She was already nervous enough about presenting her first magic show – and now this. Not that she didn't know her stuff. Her grandfather was a well-known local magician who brought joy to children of all ages and he had taught her all the tricks of his trade ever since she was a toddler.

She tried again. She covered the cane with a beautiful black cape and then with a flourish whipped it away. Nothing happened.

"It didn't work," her mother pointed out unnecessarily.

"No, it didn't!" snapped Lucy. She started pulling on the end of the cane where flowers were supposed to have magically appeared. There was a snap and suddenly Lucy held two pieces of cane instead of one. "Oh no!" she wailed, "Holly will *never* forgive me. She's counting on me. She's told all her friends, and

A for Effort

they'll be expecting a magic show at the birthday party." She flopped down in a dining room chair, tossing the now useless cane on the table. It was a key prop in *three* of her tricks.

"Not only that, Mom, I've invited Uncle Bob to come watch. I'll be so embarrassed." Uncle Bob was her most favorite person in the world, outside of Grandpa, and she had been excited about how impressed he would be.

"Now, don't fret yet, dear," her mother said. "We'll call Grandpa and see that he can do." She winked, "He's always got something up his sleeve."

"But Mom, I couldn't use his cane. It's very expensive and he needs it."

"Well, we'll see." She went over to the phone in the corner. Lucy went into the kitchen to get a drink. When she came back her mother was just hanging up.

"There," she said, "I told you. He's got an extra one and he'll bring it over tomorrow."

"That's magic!" exclaimed Lucy with relief.

After school the next day, Grandpa was already in the kitchen drinking tea with her mother when Lucy arrived home.

"So, Houdini," he said with a smile as she came in, "I hear you're having problems."

"I sure am," replied Lucy as she set her books on the table.

"Well, let's see it."

Lucy ran to get the two pieces of cane.

"You're right," he said, inspecting the cane when she came back. "This one's done for." He pulled another cane out of a bag at his feet.

"We'll try this one. But first," he said with a grin, "we'll learn how to use it again."

As Grandpa was showing Lucy how to use the cane the phone rang. Lucy's mother went into the dining-room to answer it. When she came back she stood at the door, a deeply worried expression on her face. Lucy, sensing something was wrong, looked up immediately. "What's wrong, Mom? Who was it?"

Mrs. Busby came in slowly and sat down at the kitchen table, pushing away her cup of tea. "It's your Uncle Bob, Lucy."

"Yes?" said Lucy, alarmed.

"He's coming tomorrow."

Lucy sighed with relief. "Well, of course he is, Mom. I invited him to watch the magic show. Holly said it was all right. I told you about it, remember?"

Lucy's mother stared into the cup. "He's not coming for that, Lucy."

"But he promised!"

"Lucy, Uncle Bob needs to have an emergency operation, Saturday afternoon, the day after tomorrow."

"But . . ."

Her mother reached over and took Lucy's hand. No one had to tell her how much Uncle Bob meant to Lucy. Long ago, Uncle Bob, a widower with no children, had adopted Lucy as his friend and teaching companion. Whenever he went out of town to teach he'd take her along. Sometimes they would drive as far away as 100 miles to give firesides in different communities. Uncle Bob was always in demand.

At the same time, Mrs. Busby knew she couldn't hide the truth from Lucy.

"Lucy, they say it's cancer . . ."

Lucy was so stunned she couldn't speak for a moment. She looked to her grandfather. The shock had drained the color from his face.

Finally she asked, "Is he going to die?"

Mrs. Busby hesitated. "The operation is serious." She pressed her hand. "I think you should know that."

Lucy felt like her world was caving in. She knew her uncle was old, much older than her mother – and quite fragile. But it just didn't seem possible. Uncle Bob was always there. She thought back to the times when, driving down the highway, they would sing Bahá'í songs at the top of their voices, in disjointed harmony. They would arrive at their destination filled with joy – knowing that just the "movement from place to place", as her uncle had often told her, would help the Faith in some mysterious way. It was her uncle who had taught her that even she, a child, could raise her voice and speak the name of Bahá'u'lláh – and that people *would* listen.

One solitary tear rolled down her cheek. Her grandfather solemnly reached over and gently wiped it away. He took both of her hands and turned her toward him.

"Sweetheart, listen. God may decide to take him from us, and then again maybe He won't. But you and I know that Bob has devoted his life to Bahá'u'lláh. Whatever happens he is close to His Great Heart. What could be sweeter?"

Lucy, pale and trembling, tried to smile. "I know . . ."

"But we can still pray that God will keep him with us a while longer." He looked past Lucy at his daughter who got up and came back with a prayer book. He took it and turned to the Long Healing Prayer. As he was about to begin, Lucy said timidly, "May I say it?"

And Lucy prayed – harder than she had ever

prayed before. The words rolled off her tongue, hesitantly at first and then with greater strength.

When the prayer was finished they all sat silently. Then Lucy said, "Is he still staying with us tomorrow night?"

"Yes, he's not being admitted into the hospital until the next morning."

"Then I'll call Holly and tell her that I can't come to the party."

For a moment her mother didn't answer. "Lucy" she finally said, "you promised Holly you would do this magic show a long time ago. She's counting on you."

"But this may be my last evening with Uncle Bob! How could I go knowing that? How could a stupid magic show be so important?"

"*Any* promise you make is important, dear. Holly trusts you and one of our most important duties as Bahá'ís is to be trustworthy. If we make promises we keep them, even if it's difficult. That's what being a Bahá'í means.

"But . . ."

"Uncle Bob will be here when you get home. The party starts early – 5:30. You can be home by 8:00."

Lucy's shoulders slumped. "Okay," she said reluctantly.

"And now," said Grandpa, "we can brush up on your magic act."

"Oh Grandpa, I really don't feel like it."

"It's better than moping around, isn't it?"

"I guess so."

The next evening Lucy arrived at the party on time, resplendant in her gold and black magician's costume. She had thought that she would be excited the first time she wore it, but somehow the gold stars didn't seem so bright and she felt hot. She kept thinking about Uncle Bob and when 6:30 rolled around she knew he would already be at the house.

The time for her magic show arrived. Lucy stood stiffly in front of the giggling, shoving crowd of girls and tried to smile. She raised her arms and began her act, thankful at least that her cane was working.

She worked through her tricks mechanically, one by one, calling up her delighted school friends to act as assistants. The big moment came when, to a chorus of oohs and aahs, she pulled a plump, furry rabbit from her collapsible black hat.

Then it was over.

She put the rabbit carefully back into its cage and packed up her show things in a black case. She was standing uncertainly among the laughing crowd when Holly and her mother, Mrs. Freeman, came up and thanked her.

"Come on, Lucy, it's time to cut the cake."

"I – I have to go home."

Mrs. Freeman looked at Lucy curiously. "What's the matter, Lucy? You've been acting a little strange all evening – or is that just magician's nerves?"

"No, you see . . . my Uncle Bob . . ." but then she couldn't get any further. All the pent up tears welled up and spilled out.

Mrs. Freeman looked surprised and concerned. "Let's sit down, Lucy, and you tell me all about it." She led her to the couch and Lucy, in spurts and sobs, told her story.

"You should never have come, Lucy," Holly's mother exclaimed. "Why didn't you just tell us?"

"But I – I promised. I couldn't go back on my promise . . ."

"But all that for a promise? One small promise means that much to you?"

Lucy looked up, wiping away a stray tear. "All promises are important, aren't they?"

Holly's mother studied her a moment with a strange light in her eyes. "I couldn't have said it better." Then she smiled. "Come on. I'll take you home."

"Oh no, Mrs. Freeman. I can walk. You should stay at the party. You were going to cut the cake."

"Holly can handle that herself." She put her arm around Lucy and walked to the door.

When they got to the house Mrs. Freeman came in, greeted Lucy's mother and apologized for keeping Lucy away from home on such a night. Mrs. Busby looked at Lucy's tear-stained face.

"She told us all about it – after the magic show. I'm sorry we didn't know before," Mrs. Freeman finished.

"We knew she'd get home early. She'll have plenty of time to visit with her uncle." She turned to Lucy. "He's in the guest room, honey."

Lucy was gone in a flash.

As Mrs. Freeman started to leave she noticed the Greatest Name above the door. She turned to Lucy's mother. "You're Bahá'ís?"

"Why yes, do you know about the Bahá'í Faith?"

"Yes, I had a good friend once who was a Bahá'í." Then looking at the door where Lucy had disappeared she murmured, "I should have known . . ."

"Pardon?"

"I should have known you were Bahá'ís."

"Oh, why?"

"Because of your daughter. I mean, how many children would stick to a promise at a time like this?

My Bahá'í friend was just the same. I could *always* count on her."

She pondered the Greatest Name, seemed to hesitate and then asked, "You wouldn't have anything I could read, about your religion, I mean?"

"Why, of course. Actually, we're having a meeting here tomorrow night if you'd like to come. To tell the truth we were going to call it off because of Lucy's uncle, but so many people know about it now, we couldn't possibly get hold of everyone."

"I'd love to come. What time?"

"7:30."

Mrs. Freeman left and Lucy's mother pushed the door closed behind her with a smile. She decided she wouldn't tell Lucy what her promise had done. She'd let Lucy find out for herself tomorrow night.

The next evening, as Lucy was laying out refreshments for the fireside in the kitchen, she thought about the evening before. She still regretted the time she had lost with her uncle. As it turned out, he had been very tired and went to bed early, so she hadn't seen much of him. How could a silly promise have been so important? she thought. She piled some cookies on a plate and set the lemonade in the refrigerator. Lucy and her mother were both tense with the strain of waiting for news of Uncle Bob. He had been in surgery for four hours and still there was no news from Lucy's father who was at the hospital.

Several Bahá'ís came, along with a number of seekers – Mrs. Freeman among them. Lucy was surprised to see her but was too wrapped up in her own problems to ask how she happened to be there.

When they were all seated, one of the Bahá'ís read a prayer and Mrs. Busby turned to Lucy. "Maybe you

Lucy's Magic Promise

could start us off, dear, and tell us a few things about the Bahá'í Faith."

Lucy looked at her mother in dismay. How could she expect her to speak tonight when she was so worried about Uncle Bob? Her stomach was churning and her mind was blank! What could she say?

She took a big breath and tried to think about what Uncle Bob would say. She started off slowly, talking about Progressive Revelation. But her mind was only half on it and she kept waiting for that phone call.

She named all the past Prophets: Abraham, Moses, Zoroaster, Jesus, Muhammed, Buddha and Krishna, and explained simply that they had all come from the same God and why God had sent them. After a while she noticed that Mrs. Freeman was listening carefully to every word, nodding from time to time, her eyes bright and inquisitive. This encouraged Lucy and as she concentrated on her subject her worries about Uncle Bob slipped to the back of her mind. She talked on for about ten minutes. Then, just as she was getting to the coming of Bahá'u'lláh – the phone rang!

Lucy's heart stopped, she was suddenly filled with dread. All her worries rushed back in one terrible moment.

"I'll get it!" she cried. She jumped up, leaving the guests surprised and amused.

Lucy picked up the phone in the dining room.

"Dad?"

"Lucy?"

"Yes, it's me. What happened? Is he going to be all right?"

"Darling, they think he's going to be just fine. Of course, there'll be some tests and . . ."

That's all Lucy heard. She stood there, phone in

hand, the words echoing in her mind, "They think he's going to be just fine..."

In the silence, words from the continuing fireside drifted in. Mrs. Freeman was speaking. "This is really a wonderful message. I think I've found something really special here. And to think a child made me look into it, a child who keeps her promises even when it hurts. I thought about her a long time last night."

A child? thought Lucy. Why that's me. And all because she kept a silly promise? But maybe, maybe that promise wasn't so silly after all...

"Lucy, are you there?"

With a start Lucy remembered her father on the line. "Yes, Dad, I'm here. Give Uncle Bob a big kiss from all of us, and tell him we're praying for him." She paused. "I've got to get back to the fireside, Dad."

WHAT'S A LITTLE SWEEPING?

So there we were, Mom, Dad and I, walking down the street with our little bag of books and pamphlets and a whole pile of invitations. We were going direct teaching for the first time.

Now, direct teaching was a little different from the kind of teaching we were used to. I mean, what we used to do (and still do, when we can) was to find all kinds of ways of bringing the Faith up in ordinary, everyday, garden variety conversations and wait for people to say, "What's Bahá'í?"

Like maybe someone drops an apple on the floor – you scramble to pick it up for them and as you hand it back, maybe you say, "We are all the fruits of one tree," and then, maybe they say, "That's catchy, who said *that?*" and you say, "Bahá'u'lláh!" And then, if you're really lucky, they say, "Who's Bahá'u'lláh?" and then presto! there you are, teaching the Faith.

Or maybe you're walking down the road with a Bahá'í book (the title turned out so everybody can read it) and a friend says, "Hey, what's your book about?" and you say, "What book?" You look down, "Oh, *that* book? It's about the Bahá'í Faith", and there you are teaching again.

Or *maybe* you as a person are so kind and considerate and good that your teacher asks you, "Robby, why are you so kind and considerate and good?" And you say, "Because, Miss Thompson, I am a Bahá'í!" Mom says that's the best way to teach, but for some reason it hasn't happened to me yet. I can't figure out why.

Anyway, that's what we call 'indirect teaching'. In other words, you start out talking about something else and end up talking about the Bahá'í Faith. Now, in 'direct teaching' you *start out* talking about the Faith to complete strangers. Mom says you don't have to club them over the head and say, "Have you heard of Bahá'u'lláh?" right off. She says sometimes that makes people feel uncomfortable. But maybe, for example, the LSA sets up a meeting in the neighborhood – you can hand out invitations to it. That way, well, they can just throw it away when you're not looking and they don't have to say no. Dad says it's important not to make people feel uncomfortable. And if they're interested, then they ask about the Faith.

Now, maybe you're asking, why do we direct teach? Well, I've thought about that and the reason I've come up with is that there are 5½ billion people on this earth. If you watch the news on T.V. you'll see that most of these 5½ billion people are pretty confused; like *they* don't know Bahá'u'lláh has come and they're still wandering around doing things like starting wars and making the world a miserable place where people starve to death and eat up the ozone layer and everything. *We* know this isn't going to change until *they* know about Bahá'u'lláh.

So I thought, how many people can we teach in one day if we sit around waiting for people to drop apples – or ask about that Bahá'í book we've been lugging around from place to place? I figure maybe two, maybe three. And then you gotta think about what

What's a Little Sweeping?

happens when everyone you know has already dropped an apple. I mean, how are you going to meet new people? Even if we do teach two or three people a day for one year, that makes 1,080 people. Sounds like a lot, huh? Well, after one year you still have 5,499,999,920 people around messing up the world because they don't know about Bahá'u'lláh. I figure we gotta think about new ways of going out and telling people Bahá'u'lláh has come. When you go direct teaching you meet a lot of new people.

Anyway, not only that, it was our LSA that decided we'd start direct teaching and Mom and Dad say that whenever our LSA decides something, well, we should just get up and do it.

So, like I said, there we were, walking down the street, going from house to house inviting people to this meeting, having a grand old time, I mean really – except for one thing. I didn't get to open my mouth. Not that Mom and Dad hogged all the teaching. Sometimes they'd stop, look at me and politely wait for me to say something – but then I couldn't think of anything to say that hadn't already been said. I mean, I really wanted to teach but felt kind of funny with Mom and Dad watching, especially for the first time.

So there, in the middle of the street, I stopped. Fixing my eyes on a house across the street, I announced, "I'm going in alone."

Mom looked worried. "I don't know if that's a good idea."

"Aw, Mom, the man in the last house said an eighty-year-old lady lives there. She won't mug me or anything."

Then Dad said, "Sure, let him go." Good old Dad, *he*

doesn't worry about eighty-year-old women mugging twelve-year-old boys.

So Mom said, "Okay, we'll do the house on the left and wait for you."

I took an invitation, shoved a pamphlet into my pocket and set out across the road. I noticed, as I got closer, that the house was pretty run down. The worn steps were broken and the screen on the door was hanging in shreds. I stepped around the holes, climbed on to the rickety porch and knocked. No answer. Well, that's that, I thought. My one chance to teach all alone and I have to pick a house where nobody's home. I turned to leave.

But then, just as I was making my way down the steps, I heard a noise at the door. Someone was fumbling at the lock. Finally, there was a click and the door, creaking on its hinges, opened – about three inches. A tiny wizened black face peered out at me.

"Hi!" I said. "I just wanted..."

The door opened wider, creaking even louder and drowning out my cheerful voice. The old woman inched her way forward, clutching a battered cane. Thump... thump... thump... and stopped only when her face was about two inches from mine. She was bent over almost double and I wondered how she'd made it that far.

"Hi!" I said again, a little less sure of myself. "I just..."

"So, you've finally come," she looked at me closer (if that were possible). "Kinda young... well," she turned, "I've been waiting on you."

She'd been waiting for me. I thought on that a moment. Now, it's true, I mean, I'd heard that there *were* waiting souls – like poof! Bahá'u'lláh comes down in a dream one night and tells them that God is sending them a special message and then the next day when a Bahá'í comes teaching, they become a Bahá'í on the spot. It *does* happen. But, I thought further, she'd said I was kind of young . . . *maybe* she was expecting my parents and I'd messed up some divine plan by insisting on coming alone.

I slapped my forehead. Oh no! I thought, I'd better get my parents. But by then she'd already thumped through the door and disappeared. There was nothing to do but follow her. Maybe Bahá'u'lláh would let it work out anyhow. I silently breathed the prayer, 'The Remover of Difficulties' and passed through the door behind her.

I entered a very dark room. All the curtains, tattered as they were, were closed, windows shut. It was stifling hot. As I got used to the darkness I could see that the place was one big mess. Newspapers were stacked on every surface and where there weren't newspapers, there were piles of old clothes. Dishes were scattered over the newspapers on the coffee table. The couch was being used as a makeshift bed.

I guess she saw me looking at the couch. "Been sleeping in here now. Easier. Can't get around like I used to. Bedroom's too darn far away."

And glancing at her bent figure wrapped in a faded blue housecoat, I could see that was true. I wondered how she could get around at all. Suddenly I felt very sorry – I guess I'd never felt so sorry.

Slowly I held out the invitation to her. I couldn't think what to say.

Well, she had more energy than I thought because before I knew it, she'd whipped the paper out of my hand.

"Papers, papers, they're always sending me papers. Suppose you want me to sign it."

"No, ma'am," I said. "It's just for you to read. It's an . . ."

"Well, good," she said and stuffed it into her pocket. "You can start in here. Now, these newspapers gotta be gathered up and set out by the trash. Can't lift 'um myself, can't lift nothing anymore."

Newspapers. Taken out to the trash. Hmmm . . . Shouldn't be too difficult, I thought, and I could explain about the invitation afterwards . . .

There were a *lot* of newspapers. After the fourth load I was winded. I was stacking the last armful against the trash can next to the driveway when Mom and Dad came up.

"Robby?" Mom said. "What in the world are you doing?"

Now *anybody* could see what I was doing. "Well, Mom, I'm carrying newspapers from the house to the trash." I gotta say I was embarrassed. Here I was off teaching by myself for the first time and I hadn't said word *one* about the Bahá'í Faith.

"Oh."

"I'm going back in now."

"Okay, we'll do a couple more houses and come back," she said doubtfully.

I went back in. The old woman was sitting on the couch. I was kind of glad I'd taken the newspapers out because now there was a place to sit down.

"Ma'am," I began, "about that paper I gave you . . ."

"Don't go worrying about no paper. If that social worker wants to give me a paper, she can give it herself. Can't be expecting a young boy to explain it right." She stood up. "Now, I reckon this here rug needs a good sweeping. Be better to take it out and beat it, but . . ." she studied me thoughtfully, "you

What's a Little Sweeping?

look mighty small for that. So, you'll just have to sweep it. Broom's in the kitchen."

I mulled that one over. Social worker... I had already begun to have my doubts but now it began to dawn on me that maybe Bahá'u'lláh *hadn't* visited her in a dream last night and maybe she *wasn't* expecting me *or* my parents and maybe she thought I was SOMEBODY ELSE.

Glancing at the rug which looked as if it hadn't been swept in a *long* time, I decided this was a good time to straighten out this misunderstanding.

I opened my mouth – and closed it right away. She had sunk back on the couch with a long sigh. Was she only eighty? She looked so tired and so old that somehow it didn't seem right. I mean – what's a little sweeping? I went and got the broom.

And the mop to clean the kitchen floor... and the scouring pads to clean the stove... and the dishcloth to wash what must have been a week's worth of dishes.

I *didn't* get to the dusting, the dirty windows or the piles of old clothes because, just as I was wiping down the kitchen counter, there was a knock on the door. I threw the dish towel over my shoulder and went to answer it. I figured I could do it faster than she could.

I opened the door and there before me were two very worried parents.

"Robby?" Mom said, looking at the dish towel uncertainly.

"Hi, Mom!"

"What *have* you been doing? We finished all the houses on this street and have been standing outside here for half an hour."

"Uh... why don't you come in and meet... her?" I *still* didn't know her name.

They came in.

"Mrs... uh... these are my parents."

The old woman sat up and looked them over. "Well, have a seat," she mumbled.

Mom and Dad sat down on the now newspaper-free armchairs. I could tell they didn't quite know what to say.

"Well, Mrs..."

"Haney, Eleanor Haney."

"Well, Mrs. Haney, do you have any more questions?"

Mrs. Haney looked puzzled. Can't say that I blamed her. I decided it was time to explain to them that I hadn't gotten around to mentioning the Faith yet. But before I could open my mouth, Mrs. Haney's face lit up.

"Oh, you mean about this here paper." She pulled the crumpled invitation from her pocket.

"Yes, that's it," said Mom. "I guess you've had a lot of questions about the Bahá'í Faith."

"The what?"

"The Bahá'í Faith."

"That some religion?"

Mom looked at me. I smiled innocently – there wasn't much else I could do.

"Yes, the Bahá'í Faith is a religion. Hasn't Robby been telling you about it?"

"He didn't say nothing about no religion." She peered up at me. "You come here to talk about the Lord, young man?"

"Yes, Ma'am."

She thought about that. "... And you're not that

boy the social worker promised to send round to help me about the house?"

"Uh, no Ma'am."

She chuckled. "Well, I'll be doggoned," she said and she chuckled again. In fact, she chuckled so much her whole body shook and I began to worry maybe she'd fall off the couch. But soon she stopped chuckling and shaking and leaned back to catch her breath.

When she sat back she leaned toward me. "All right, young man, what you got to tell me about religion that I don't already know."

"Well," I answered immediately, "I know that Bahá'u'lláh has come."

But she seemed not to have heard me. "That's fine. Now let me tell you what religion is – religion is doing, not talking. You gotta help people. Talking about the Lord is no good unless you help someone too." She leaned back again and pondered that a moment.

I did too. I mean, I guessed that I'd been pretty much 'doing' all afternoon.

She chuckled again. "Guess that's what you've been pretty much doing all afternoon."

"I've been trying, Ma'am."

"Polite too, aren't you. Not like these good-for-nothing young scamps always hanging around who don't know what respect for an old woman is..." She paused. "All right, where you all hold your meetings?"

"We're having a meeting at the Community Center, just down the street, tomorrow night – 7:30."

"That's not like a real church, but..." she eyed my parents, "You'll pick me up?"

"We'd be happy to," Mom answered.

"Well, all right, I'll give it a try. I don't hold much

A for Effort

with these so-called new religions, but if you're talking about the Lord... and cleaning people's houses..." She peered at me again, "You'll be back next week?"

Would I be back next week? I looked at the dirty windows, the undusted furniture and the piles of old clothes with a sigh. "Yes, Ma'am."

We all stood up to leave, saying our good-byes in the living room and left Mrs. Haney sitting on the couch.

On the walk outside Dad winked and said with a grin, "Well, young man. Looks like you've got your 'doing' cut out for you."

"Yeah," I said, glancing at the uncut lawn in the gathering dusk. Direct teaching wasn't what I had expected, but then, Bahá'u'lláh never said it'd be easy. Besides, I thought, remembering Mrs Haney's bent figure in her faded blue housecoat, it beats waiting for people to drop apples any time.

THE SHAWL AND THE BOOK

"Laura! Are you coming?"

"Sure, but . . ."

"Well, come on then! We only have fifteen minutes!"

"Jita wants to play too," called Laura.

"She doesn't know how to play. Come on!"

Laura slowly left her friend to join the others in their new game. Jita looked on despondently. She was a new girl from India and it was true, she didn't know how to play many of their games.

"We could teach her," mumbled Laura as she joined the group.

"We don't have time," said Debby. "Here, you first."

When recreation was over and they trooped back to class, Laura noticed that Jita had come in before the others. Jita sat down quickly and shoved something into her desk.

Laura, who sat near Jita, leaned over to speak to her. But Jita hissed back, "You're just like all the others."

Laura was hurt, but also a bit angry. Didn't she see that I tried to help her? Laura said to herself.

The rest of the morning Jita was very unpleasant and Laura wondered why she had ever tried to be her friend. She's strange, she thought uncomfortably.

A for Effort

Laura was a Bahá'í and she knew there were different kinds of people in the world. She knew she should try to be friends with everyone, even if they were different. How many times had her mother explained that she should look at their good qualities? "When you meet people who are different from you it makes the world more interesting. Try to love them," her mother would say.

Well, she had tried, hadn't she? Or had she?

At lunch, Laura sat down beside Jita. She was very quiet and wasn't eating. Finally she drew out what seemed to be some greasy bread and dipped it in a sauce in a small plastic container.

"What are you eating, Jita?" Laura asked.

Jita smiled slyly and offered her a piece. "Here, try some."

Laura was so happy that she was finally getting somewhere and to please Jita she took a big bite. After a couple of seconds she felt her mouth burning. She gasped and spit out the food.

Jita laughed, "Oh, is it too hot for you?"

"My new dress! Just look at it!"

There was a big yellow stain down the front of Laura's dress. Jita did look sorry and stopped laughing, but Laura was still angry. "What a mean trick!"

Neither of the girl's spoke to each other for the rest of the day. Jita seemed to grow quieter and Laura just thought, she's strange, she's different. You can't trust her. That's all there is to it!

When the bell rang and the children got up to leave, Debby cried out, "My purse! Someone's stolen my purse!"

Everyone looked around. Laura's eyes rested on Jita. What had she hidden in her desk after recreation? She *was* hiding something.

The Shawl and the Book

Jita didn't seem to have heard Debby's cry. She was putting things into her school bag, but in such a way that no one could see exactly what she was doing.

Could she be the one? thought Laura. Did she come in before the end of recreation, steal the purse and hide it in her desk, just as I came in?

Laura thought about it again that evening and later, before bed, she told her mother about it.

"Well," said her mother, "did you see her take it?"

"No, but she must be the one!"

"Laura, if you don't know for sure you mustn't say a word about this."

"But I know, Mom!"

"You *don't* know, Laura. She could have put something else in her desk that she didn't want others to see."

"I don't know," Laura sighed. "Well, okay, I won't say anything."

The next morning on the way to school, Laura met Debby. "Did you find your purse?"

"No, it was stolen. I know it. Who do you think would take it?"

Laura, remembering her mother's words, answered, "Maybe you lost it, Debby."

"I didn't lose it, I tell you! Who would have taken it? You didn't see anyone hiding anything did you?"

"Well," mumbled Laura.

"Well what? Did you see anything suspicious?"

"Well nothing!" Laura answered.

Debby stopped and grabbed Laura's shoulders. "You *did* see something! Now tell me!"

"Well, you know that Jita was angry with us..."

"Jita!" exclaimed Debby. "Of course – who else could it be? What did you see?"

Laura felt terrible, but the words tumbled out, "She was in the class after recreation, before the others came in, and I saw her shove something in her desk – like she was hiding something."

"So!" cried Debby.

They had arrived at school and Debby went immediately to find the other girls in the class. Laura could see them whispering and glancing at Jita. She knew what they were saying and she knew that she was the cause of it.

Throughout the morning, no one looked or spoke to Jita. She seemed to sense something was wrong and looked bewildered and became even quieter than usual.

At recreation Jita carried her school bag out into the schoolyard. She opened it several times to touch what was inside, but no one could see what she had. This made the girls whisper even more furiously to each other.

Laura couldn't join in the games; she could only watch Jita. Jita looked so alone, Laura thought. *So what if she did steal the purse? Maybe she hasn't got one of her own? What have I done to her?*

Laura felt tears stinging in her eyes as they all walked back to class. It was the longest day she had ever spent. By the end of the day, it was clear that everyone knew about Jita and the stolen purse.

Just before the bell rang, Debby stood up. "Miss Adams, may I say something?"

"Yes, Debby," the teacher answered. "What is it?"

"Yesterday I told you that my purse was missing. Laura saw Jita in the classroom alone during recreation and saw her hide something in her desk.

The Shawl and the Book

Again today Jita seems to be hiding something in her bag. It's my purse. I know it and I want to have it back."

There was a deadly silence in the classroom.

"Jita, is this true? Do you have Debby's purse?"

Jita said nothing.

The teacher got up and walked to her desk. "Give me your bag, Jita."

She gave Miss Adams the bag without a word, and Miss Adams emptied it on the desk.

There was no stolen purse. There, lying on the desk, was what looked like a very old, beautifully colored book and a delicate purple shawl.

"Is this what you were hiding?" the teacher asked softly.

Jita looked up at Miss Adams through the tears in her eyes.

"My mother gave it to me before I left India – she couldn't come with us. When I . . . when I want to remember her, I like to look at them."

The bell rang loudly and at that moment an older boy walked in. "I have a message from the office. It seems that Debby Draper left something in the schoolyard during recreation yesterday and they want her to come pick it up."

No one moved or spoke except Debby, who slowly gathered her things and started to leave.

"Just a moment, Debby," said the teacher. "I think we can all apologize to Jita now."

Again no one moved. "Please," said Jita, "it's no one's fault."

"Yes it is," said Laura. "It's my fault. I was the one who accused her and I want to say that I'm sorry."

"And Debby?" asked the teacher.

"I'm sorry too."

When they had all left, Laura stayed behind as Jita rearranged her school bag. Laura wanted to speak but the words wouldn't come. Finally she managed, "What can I say, Jita?"

Jita turned and faced her. "Maybe you could say that we're friends."

Laura held out her hand with a smile, "It's a deal!"

Laura never told her mother what happened that day in class. All her mother knew was that Laura had a new friend. She would smile to herself when she saw the two girls, one black head and one blond, bent over a beautifully colored book from India.

"And in this story," Jita would explain, "Lord Krishna tells the people that they should love Him . . ."

AFRICAN BLUES

"Well, Nicky boy, that's it, everything's unpacked," Mom announced. "Wouldn't you like to go out now? I saw some nice boys on the road looking in the gate."

"No," I said. That was about the hundredth time I'd said it too. No one was going to push me out that door, not even Mom, who had to be *the* expert pusher. Mom plopped down on our new chair and sighed. That was about the hundredth time she'd sighed too.

"Why not?"

"Don't want to."

"Why?" she repeated. Wasn't she ever going to get tired of that word? "Once you get out more you'll find some friends and be playing up a storm as usual. It's not like you to be shy!" She sighed again.

"I don't speak French. They won't understand me."

"But you can *learn* French. Lots of people learn French every day!"

"Don't want to learn French. They'd just laugh at me. Anyway . . ." I stopped. Mom was altogether too nosy.

"Yes?"

"Nothing."

"Anyway what?"

Didn't she ever give up? I sighed. "Anyway they're different."

"Different?" Mom mused.

"They're black."

She paused, shocked. "I can't believe you said that — lots of your best Bahá'í friends in the States are black."

"They're very black."

"What difference does 'very black' make?" She was exasperated now. I could tell. But then suddenly she smiled. She got up and came to me, putting her hands on my shoulders. "Dear... ," she began. Lovey dovey, that's how she got when everything else failed. "Dear Nick," she pressed her nose against mine until they were both flat. She was being unfair. She knew that always made me laugh. But it wasn't going to work. Not this time. "Dear Nicky, what's the difference?"

I pulled away. Getting my nose back to it's proper shape put things in better perspective. "They're very black and they speak a stupid language I don't understand and they eat funny things with their *hands* and they..." I dropped down on a chair beside her. This was ridiculous. I always had to *explain*. She always had to get in my mind and understand. What was there to understand? I didn't want to go out. Period.

"Oh!" she murmured. "I understand." Her face lit up. "Culture shock!"

Good grief. She had a name for everything. The game's lost, I told myself miserably, she *understands*! I got up in one bound and headed toward the door.

"Where are you going?" She asked startled.

"Out!"

"Oh," she almost sounded disappointed.

I smiled to myself as I let the screen door slam shut

behind me. "Culture shock," I muttered. No way was I going to listen to an explanation of that!

I wandered around the yard for a few minutes, kicking a tree here and there, uprooting a plant or two. Stupid plants, why couldn't they make plants here like at home. Everything had to be so different. They uprooted me just like this plant. I tore it in two. No one asked *me*! They just packed up my toys, giving away half of them in the process ("You're getting too old for *that*"). Had me say good-bye to my lifelong friends ("Say goodbye *nicely*, dear") and poof, there we were on a plane to *West Africa* of all places.

Sure, Mom and Dad explained that now we were pioneers. But we were already pioneers in Kansas – homefront pioneers. And we were doing just fine.

Before I could pull up another plant, I stopped. There was a rattle at the gate. There they were again, those boys. Speaking gibberish and grinning like fools. I'd show 'um. I charged the gate with a terrifying expression and ran into it with a bang. They backed off and looked at me curiously. They didn't look terrified. Before I could find another sure fire way to scare them off, one of them pointed to a tree behind me.

"Badam," he said.

"Badam," echoed the other.

"Badam," I repeated stupidly.

They pointed again. I unlatched the gate. I'd see what they wanted and *then* really scare them off.

Suddenly they were inside throwing rocks at the tree. Good grief, I thought to myself. So, is this some kind of evil tree that they have to throw rocks at?

Then I noticed some things had fallen from the tree. The boys grabbed them and stuffed them into their pockets. I bent over and examined one they missed. It look like a small oblong green fruit, but was hard and didn't look edible.

The boys, spouting gibberish all the time, took their hoard to the road just outside the gate. One of them grabbed a big rock and smashed a green "fruit". It broke open. I didn't see what was inside because it was instantly in his mouth.

Fine thing, I thought. Could have offered *me* one.

At that very instant, I guess one of the boys noticed that I was staring rather stupidly at the whole process. He grinned, brought his rock down hard and broke open another "fruit". He quickly pulled out a thin long nut and handed it to me. He grinned again. "*Manges*," he said.

Well, I *did* know enough French to understand *that* and obediently popped it into my mouth. Not bad, I thought as I crunched down. Almost like almonds. But when I tried to swallow it, it got stuck in my throat. It didn't *go down* like almonds. I must have started to turn red with the effort and the next thing I knew they were both pounding me on the back and pretty soon after that a squashy brown and white mess was laying in the dust. The boys thought this was hilarious.

I didn't. I got up, went back inside the gate and slammed it behind me. Stupid kids. Jabber, jabber, jabber. They left.

I wandered around the yard a bit after that and then tried my hand at knocking "badams" from the tree. Not having anything else to do I picked them up, brought them to the porch and found myself a big rock. Just as I was bringing it down on the first one, Mom stuck her head out the door.

"Made some friends, didn't you?"

This was too much. Now she was *spying* on me!

"No!" I barked and succeeded in bashing my badam to bits, nut and all.

She watched me a moment and then said, "I just got a call from an American lady. She only lives a few houses away. She has a son your age and you're invited to play there tomorrow."

"Anything's better than these stupid kids," I grumbled.

Mom just stood there looking at me. I knew what she was thinking, and she knew I knew what she was thinking.

"I don't know Nicky, maybe you'll feel differently after a while." She sighed, "Well, we'll just have to wait and see. Anyway, lunch is ready."

"What's for lunch?" I asked, glumly brushing all the badams off the porch in one sweep.

She smiled, "Tuna fish."

"Tuna fish? Where'd you get that?" This was a surprise.

"Brought it with us, been saving it for a rainy day."

"It's not raining," I reminded her.

"I know, but I didn't count on the dry season. Anyway it's ready, unless of course you'd like me to freeze your part until the rainy season rolls around."

"All right, all right!" I sighed.

One good thing about living in Africa was that Dad was always home for lunch and didn't go back to work until three. Siesta time.

We ate our tuna fish. I savored every bite. Usually nothing seemed to taste right here. Even the mayonnaise from France tasted funny and the French mustard burned your mouth. But Mom, full of surprises, had come up with some American mayonnaise and mild mustard.

I was wondering what else she might have stashed

away when my dad cleared his throat. Now, when Dad clears his throat, it means he's going to say something important. I looked up.

"Nick..."

I was right. "Yeah?"

"Your mom says you're a little depressed..."

"Yeah," I said.

He looked at me a moment and then he said, "Well, let's have it."

I hesitated, looking down at my plate. Then I took a big breath. "O.K., it's just that there we were in Kansas, doing fine, I had lots of friends – I was doing well in school – you had lots of people coming to firesides... I mean, I even brought my teacher to one – and then poof! We all have to go flying off to Africa. We don't know anything about these people; we don't even speak French. For Pete's sake, we don't even know how to say 'fireside' in French – what's the good in being here?"

Mom pushed her plate away, brushing some crumbs into her hand. "Nicky, you're right. What you say may be true now..." She paused. "But you've got to think about what being a Bahá'í is all about. First of all, why do you think Bahá'u'lláh came?"

"Well, I guess to teach us how to live..."

"And," Mom said, "to live in unity."

"But we can do that a lot better in America where we know people, where we fit in."

"That's just the point." Dad interrupted. "Bahá'u'lláh didn't come just to bring Americans together – He came to bring the whole world together. Look, here we have a perfect chance to put what we believe to the test. We may say that we love mankind – but can we love our African neighbors..." he smiled, "even if they *do* eat with their hands?"

I realized I hadn't thought much about that. I blushed and shifted uncomfortably in my chair.

"Now don't get all embarrassed. Your Mom and I have similar problems. It's not easy for us either."

"But you know Nicky," Mom continued, "that's not the only reason we're pioneers. We're pioneers because Bahá'u'lláh says that it's the most wonderful thing we can do. He says it's the 'most meritorious of all deeds.' So, when your dad and I read that, we decided that it was right for us.

"We did think about it for a long time. First, we thought, what is the most important thing in our lives? The answer we came up with was to know and love God. Then we thought about what was the best way to know and love God. And we decided that it was to follow *everything* in the Bahá'í writings. From the writings we learned that the most important thing to do now was to teach the Faith and to build the new kingdom of God on earth. And *then*, after reading, we decided that the most meritorious way to teach the Faith was to leave our country and pioneer."

"That's right," said Dad. "Even if we don't know the people here, even if we can't speak the language yet, we know that it will all work out in the end. Bahá'u'lláh wouldn't tell us to do something if He weren't going to help us, would He?"

"No, I guess not . . ." I said, dabbing at the crumbs on my plate. It began to make sense and I wondered why I hadn't brought it all up before. I suppose I was too busy being sulky. "So," I said, "I guess I gotta get used to the idea."

"It would help," Dad said grinning. Then he looked at me for a moment, his grin fading, "I guess this is our fault in a way. Mom and I should have talked with you more about it before we left. We should have prepared you more. Anyway, we'll do what we can to help you. We're all in this together, Nick."

"Yeah," I said, trying to sound convinced, and took my dishes to the sink.

After lunch I wandered out again. Nothing else to do. School wouldn't start for two months. I thought about what Mom and Dad had said. It *did* make sense. I mean, if Bahá'u'lláh said it, who was I to argue? But still . . . maybe I could just love Africans without talking to them.

Only a few minutes had passed when, through the fence, I noticed what I thought were the same two boys walking by. I couldn't be sure, but I looked closer, pressing my face against the fence. One of the boys had an old tire with two sticks stuck inside it and was rolling it along the ground. That's something new, I thought to myself. The other boy had a large car which he was pushing with a stick. It was made of light plywood. Hand made, I thought, but not a bad job.

They must have seen me through the fence because they stopped. One of them motioned with his hand, "*Viens!*" he said. Well, this too was part of my limited French vocabulary and meant "come". I thought about it and then unlatched the gate and stepped outside. Nothing to lose. The boy with the tire stuck the two sticks in my hand and off we went down the street, me awkwardly rolling the silly tire.

A few houses down the road, we turned into a courtyard. In the center, there were clothes stretched out on the ground to dry. It seemed a pretty risky way to dry clothes to me. Kids were running around all over the place. There was a crumbling lean-to in the corner with no walls, just a tin roof on poles, and inside there was a woman. She had a baby tied to her back with a piece of cloth and was bending over a cooking pot. The pot was resting on three large stones and a wood fire had been built underneath. One of the boys called to the woman and she looked at me in surprise. Then she smiled, so I guessed I was welcome. Maybe it's his mother, I thought.

Then she took a tin plate, loaded some rice on it and topped it with red sauce containing a few small pieces of meat. She barked out an order and the two boys, along with a smaller child, all ran to a bucket and washed their hands. Then she handed a plate to one of the boys, who sat on the ground with the others. They all dug in, eating from the same plate with their hands. It didn't look all that appetizing and I decided maybe I should go now since it was their lunch time and all. Then the woman took out a clean china plate, wiped it off with what looked like a clean towel and handed it to me. She motioned to one of the boys, who immediately got up and brought a low table and stool. Then she loaded a big portion on to my plate and told me to sit down. (I understood her too – maybe my French *wasn't* so bad.)

You might guess that I was beginning to feel uneasy by now, not knowing exactly what was in that sauce. I mean, it could have been monkey or . . . or anything. Besides that, my tuna fish hadn't settled any too well. But the lady smiled so sweetly there was nothing left to do but dig in. Luckily she'd provided me with a fork. All I can say is that it was a good thing I had a Mexican aunt who'd stuffed me with hot peppers since I was two, because the stew was full of them. My eyes watered, my nose ran and

A for Effort

I looked around frantically for water. It arrived in a small calabash (drinking gourd).

So there I was, with kids running all around, chickens squawking, the baby crying, my nose running and the lady smiling at me all the time, while she kind of hopped up and down to quiet the baby. I ate and ate and as I scraped up the last few grains of rice I thought my stomach would burst. I got up, none too steadily on my feet, and delivered what I thought was a very fluent "*Merci!*" and started to leave.

Just then, one of the boys hopped to his feet. "*Attends*," he said and ran off into one of the rooms that led off the courtyard. I assumed this meant "wait". He was back in a few seconds carrying his homemade plywood car. I thought he meant to accompany me home and was planning to push his car along. But to my surprise he pushed the car into my hands.

"Yannick," he said. I thought he was talking about the car, but then saw he was pointing to himself. Then he pointed to his brother, "Yves," he said.

I pointed to myself, "Nick."

They repeated, "Nick" and grinned.

I grinned too, not knowing what to say, even if I knew how to say it. So I came out with my famous "*Merci*" and walked home, leaving the squawking chickens, the baby and the bubbling cooking pot behind.

"Where on earth did you get that?" asked Mom when she saw the car.

"Yannick gave it to me."

She brightened immediately. "An African friend?"

"Yeah," I said. That should make her happy. Then she looked worried.

"Maybe you shouldn't have taken it. I mean, what if it was his only toy?"

"Mom, there was nothing else I could do. He put it in my hands. It would have, have . . ."

"Have what?"

"It would have hurt his feelings!"

Mom thought about that. She always thought about everything. "Well then, it was a noble thing to do, Nicky."

Noble now, get off it. I did what I had to. "Yeah."

The next day was "American' day. I ate breakfast, got dressed and said prayers with Mom and Dad. Then I set off for the "American" house.

Mrs. Crocker opened the door. "Well isn't this nice, Nicky. You've come to play with my Timmy. He'll be so happy. He's been so alone."

"Thank you, Mrs. Crocker."

'Timmy' was found in his room playing with an enormous toy garage, loaded with about fifty miniature cars and trucks. He stood up as I came in.

"Boy am I happy to see you. I guess you speak real English."

"I guess so." I said.

"Yeah, well I'm really sick and tired of everyone jabbering at me in French."

Don't ask me why I said it, but out it came, "Well you *can* learn French, you know. It's easy."

"You speak French?" he asked in amazement.

"I can understand a few words," I said smugly.

"Well, I'm not even going to try. It's a stupid language."

He picked up what looked like a brand new truck and zoomed it around the room a few times. Then he settled down beside me. "You're new here. I don't suppose you've met any African kids yet."

"I've met a few."

"Well I've seen them. Mom says they eat with their hands."

"So, you eat sandwiches with a fork?"

"Oh, you know what I mean!"

"Yeah well, maybe I do."

"And they're so poor they have to make their own toys. I saw this one guy yesterday. He went right by the house with some stupid looking car that looked like he nailed it together himself."

"Oh?" I said casually, thinking about the car I left on my bedroom dresser.

"Anyway, I'm glad you're here. We can have some real fun."

So we played for a while and I stayed for lunch. Peanut butter. American peanut butter with grape jelly. They had a whole pantry full.

The next morning Mom was hanging out the laundry while I sat on the porch trying to decide what to do.

"Why don't you go over to Timmy's?" She suggested. "They invited you again today. Then maybe you can bring him home for lunch."

"Yeah." I didn't move.

"You do like Timmy, don't you?"

"He's okay."

"Well?"

Well what? Always pushing. I'd go when I wanted. Always rush, rush, rush. I still didn't move.

Mom gave up and concentrated on her laundry.

There was a rattle at the gate. I sat up and peered through the metal slats. There stood Yannick and Yves. Looking closer, I saw they both had homemade fishing poles over their shoulders. Yannick was holding a rusty metal can.

"Looks like your friends are here," Mom said.

"Yeah." I stood up.

"Looks like they're going fishing."

"Yeah." I went to unlatch the gate.

"*Rivière*," said Yannick and pointed down the road.

"I unpacked your fishing pole. It's in your closet," Mom called out.

"Yeah." I called back. Turning to the boys I held up one finger, "*Une minute!*"

They nodded, they understood!

And I ran to get my fishing pole.

A TIME FOR EVERYTHING

Carrie slammed her math book shut in frustration, picked it up and marched out of her room, her dark curls flouncing with every step.

"Mom!" she called. She stopped short when she saw her mother, coat in hand, ready to walk out the door.

"Where are *you* going?" she asked sulkily.

"Honey, you know I have an LSA meeting tonight."

"But I need help with my math!" She threw herself into an armchair in exasperation.

"Don't worry, sweetheart; Dad's in the study, you can ask him." She put on her coat. "I'll be a bit late tonight. We're working out the last details of the teaching project."

"Yeah," mumbled Carrie. She drew her jean-clad knees up to her chin and regarded her mother gloomily.

Carrie's mom looked at her a moment. Then she came over and gently kissed her cheek. "We're all looking forward to this project — even you were excited yesterday about going out teaching with the youth all alone for the first time. But something like this takes a lot of work." She smiled. "Tomorrow I'll have a look at that math — go see your dad now."

"Okay," Carrie said, a bit mollified. It was true she was excited about the teaching project. Up until that time she'd always gone out teaching with her parents. Most of the time they'd taught adults and Carrie really didn't have much to say. This time, even though she was only twelve, she'd go out with the youth and her parents wouldn't be there. It scared her just a little bit, but still she was happy. "Just depend on Bahá'u'lláh and open your mouth," her dad would often say.

She watched with a sigh as her mom quietly left and then popped her head around the door of the study where her father was busy banging away on the computer.

"Dad," she began.

"Just a minute, honey, let me finish this paragraph." He typed on for a few minutes. She noticed that his once black hair was streaked with grey now. He turned around and his clear blue eyes and unlined face made him look much younger. "Yes?"

"Dad, I don't understand this math. Could you help me?"

"Gee, sweetie, I've got this report to get out tonight." Her dad was an Auxilliary Board Member and *always* seemed to be writing reports. "Look, we'll set aside some time tomorrow and take a good look at it."

Carrie didn't say anything. The words were on the tip of her tongue, "My math test *is* tomorrow!" But she held back. She just stood there as her father turned back around, frowning at his papers.

Nobody ever has time for *me*, she thought. Deepenings, Feasts, firesides, reports – there was all the time in the world for these things but none for her.

Her fingers tightened around her math book until her knuckles showed white and she walked out of the room. Back in her bedroom, she threw her book down

A Time for Everything

on the desk and got ready for bed. She slipped between the cool sheets and squeezed her eyes shut in the darkness. She didn't pray – the prayers just wouldn't come.

The next morning at breakfast, she found her mom in the kitchen wrapped in an old robe. She looked fresh and cheerful as usual. Carrie's mood had not improved and when her mother said, "You missed prayers this morning, dear," she merely murmured, "I was tired."

Her mother served her biscuits and juice while Carrie poured cereal into her bowl. She added the milk but then, instead of eating, she just stared into her bowl.

"Did you finish your report, Dad?" she asked abruptly.

Her dad looked up from his newspaper. "Yes, I did – at 1:00 a.m.!"

"And you, Mom, did you have a good meeting?"

"Yes, we got a lot done."

"Well, that's very good," said Carrie, carefully replacing the biscuit in the serving dish and pushing her bowl away. "Because I'm going to fail a math test today."

Carrie's mother and father looked at each other for a moment. Then her mom spoke, "Carrie, you didn't tell us you had a math test *today*."

"No one seemed interested," said Carrie as she pushed her chair back and got up.

"Carrie, sit and talk for a minute," said her father gently as he put his newspaper aside.

Carrie sat down, trying not to look into their eyes. Her own were rapidly filling with tears.

"I think we should have a nice long consultation about this," Mom announced. "What about tonight?"

"Good idea," said Dad.

"Okay," said Carrie, managing a faint smile through her tears.

That evening after dinner, Carrie and her parents settled in the living room for consultation. This wasn't unusual. They often set aside times to consult when there were problems. But Carrie wasn't feeling up to it. She hadn't had time to sort out her feelings. She felt confused and hurt and sat curled up in a corner of the sofa as far away from her parents as she could.

"Why don't you say the Tablet of Aḥmad, Carrie?"

Carrie was in *no* mood for the Tablet of Aḥmad, but she sulkily crossed her arms and recited it as quickly as she could, stumbling over words she normally knew perfectly. Her mother softly corrected her from time to time.

When she finished, there was a moment of silence. Her father looked faintly amused. "Well, we didn't waste any time on *that* prayer, did we?"

Carrie blushed.

"How'd you do on your math test?"

"We exchanged papers and corrected it in class." She stopped short and then blurted out, "I got a 'C'."

"Not as good as usual, but you'll make it up." Her father paused. "Carrie, I guess you feel we're not paying enough attention to you. Is that right?"

"I guess so," mumbled Carrie as she settled further into her corner of the couch. Then she suddenly sat up straight. "It's just that the last two weekends I've had to call Mary's mother to get a ride to dance lesson because Mom's been gone. It's embarrassing. I

A Time for Everything

wanted to go to the library but nobody had time to take me. And now, now no one has time to help me with my math! Everyone seems to have time for Bahá'u'lláh, but no time for me!"

Her mom sat very still. When Carrie glanced up she was surprised to see her mother's eyes were brimming with tears. Then she spoke. "I know Carrie, I've had District Teaching Committee two weekends in a row preparing for our two new projects, and because our LSA is participating in the projects I've been doubly busy these past couple of weeks. But don't think I haven't worried about you. Every time I go out that door I think of you, honey. Not just during these past two weeks, but all your life I've tried to figure out how to do my duty to Bahá'u'lláh and still be a good parent."

Her father broke in, "You know last year we went to the LSA just to ask advice about how we could serve the Faith and still take good care of you."

Carrie lowered her head, "I didn't know."

"Carrie," her mother began, "how often you've said that you wished you had lived in the time of the Báb or Bahá'u'lláh. How you would have liked to have been one of those early heroes like Zaynab or Mullá Ḥusayn. Well, darling the time for heroes isn't over. Has the world accepted Bahá'u'lláh yet?"

"No, Mom, I know it hasn't. That's why we teach."

"Right. After many years as a Bahá'í, I've only just come to see that this new world order of Bahá'u'lláh isn't going to be handed to us on a silver platter. We have to work, sacrifice and teach. I think sacrifice is the key – when we sacrifice our time for the Faith, it's just like Zaynab was sacrificing her very blood. How else is the world going to become Bahá'í? Who else can teach but we Bahá'ís? So, honey, if your mom always seems to be busy it's because she's trying to be a hero in her own small way."

"But," Dad added, "that doesn't mean we don't love and take care of our little girl."

"That's right, and we try. I know it's been a bit of a mess these past two weeks, but we're going to try harder. You mean everything to us."

Carrie, her head still lowered, picked at the lint on the sofa. "I know you're right, Mom, it's just that . . ."

"That we've been pretty busy lately and haven't taken proper care of you," her dad finished. "Well, maybe we can work on that. First of all, I suggest that you let us know ahead of time when you're going to have a test, or even when you're having problems, and we'll make *sure* one of us sits down with you to help. If I had known last night that your math test was today, I would have helped you and finished my report early this morning.

"And," he continued, "I think we should have a regular consultation time. Let's say Sunday night. That way we can work out any problems *before* they get too serious."

"Another thing," said her mom thoughtfully. "It occurred to me that you might like to help me sometimes. Like the Bahá'í library work I do. Why, you could count books, help fill out forms, any number of things that would give me more time for you."

"I'd like that," said Carrie, brushing away the pile of lint she'd collected. She smiled timidly, "If you really think I could help . . ."

"And we can get to that math right now," her father said.

"I'll get my book," she jumped up, but remembering something else turned to her mother. "By the way,

Mom, my new friend Monica is coming by tomorrow afternoon."

"Good, I'd like to meet her. I'm making cookies for Feast, so you'll have a treat to share with her."

The next afternoon, Carrie and Monica sat at the end of Carrie's bed munching away.

"These are great!" Monica exclaimed after swallowing an enormous bite. "Did your mother make them?"

"Yes, they're our favorites."

"You're lucky."

"Why?"

"My mom never has time to make things for us."

"Oh, does she work?"

"No, but there's her bridge club, garden club – you know, always something. She just never has time."

Carrie wondered about that. Her mom belonged to about ten different committees, but she always seemed to have some special treat in the house.

Monica crunched away, managing to devour most of the cookies set out on the plate at the end of the bed. She brushed the crumbs from Carrie's white silk bedspread.

"Carrie," she announced abruptly, "I've got a problem."

"What is it?"

"Well, you see, I've got a friend and *she's* got a problem."

"Yeah, what?"

"She stole something... a very expensive necklace."

Carrie suddenly felt uncomfortable. "What did she do that for?"

"Oh, she's always stealing things. Anyway, this time she was afraid her parents would find it, so she

A for Effort

brought it over to *my* house. Now, I'm afraid *my* parents will find it. What would *you* do?"

"Why, I guess I'd tell my parents. They always know what to do when there's a problem."

Monica looked at her with total amazement. "Tell your *parents*? Are you crazy? They'd call the police!"

Carrie hesitated and then said, "I don't think that would be the first thing they'd do at all. I think they'd consult about it and find some other way to solve the problem. But even if they did call the police in the end, well, it would be because they thought it would be the right thing to do." She paused. "Wouldn't you tell your parents?"

"I don't tell my parents anything. They never understand... anyway, they don't have time to listen. I told you, my mother never has time."

"Oh, Monica, I'm sure she has time for your problems."

Monica looked at Carrie curiously. "You know Carrie," she said, "I think your parents must be very different, because you just don't understand. My parents don't talk to me about *anything* important so I don't talk to them."

Carrie thought that over. When she really had a problem her parents always had time, even if sometimes, like lately, they got very busy, time would eventually be made for her.

"Monica," she asked, "why do you keep friends who steal?"

Monica shrugged her shoulders again. "Nobody's perfect."

"But Monica, a thief? You can get into trouble hanging around with people who aren't honest." Carrie had a hard time understanding this. She had always been raised to choose her friends carefully.

She remembered the Hidden Word she had recited that very morning at prayer time. *"The company of the ungodly increaseth sorrow, whilst fellowship with the righteous cleanseth the rust from off the heart . . ."* She looked at Monica and questioned the choice she herself had made.

"Anyway," persisted Monica, "I asked you what *you* would do, not your parents."

"Well," Carrie said slowly, "first I'd probably pray about it. Have you tried to pray about it?"

Monica opened her eyes wide in surprise. "Pray? What does praying have to do with it? Do you think God's going to come down and give me the answer – just like that?" She frowned. "Anyway, I never learned to pray."

"Your parents never taught you to pray?"

Monica laughed out loud. "My father doesn't even believe in God. Why would they teach me to pray?"

Carried considered that. She knew, of course, that there were lots of people who didn't believe in God and who had never prayed. But to her it seemed so strange. She couldn't imagine a day in her life without prayer. She thought about the many hours her parents had spent patiently teaching her to memorize prayers – the days she would look up after prayers and gaze at the picture of 'Abdu'l-Bahá on her living room wall, and how peaceful she felt. She thought of all the people like Monica who had never had that, who had never experienced a moment of prayer. And she thought of how her parents had taken the time to give it to her, day after day. She also remembered looking up from her lint gathering and seeing her mother's eyes brimming with tears. Mom really tried, and even if sometimes she was too busy for her, it wasn't because of a garden club!

A for Effort

"Well?"

Carrie looked up and saw Monica staring at her strangely. "Well, what?"

"After you pray, *then* what would you do?"

Carrie pulled herself back to the present problem. "I'd take the necklace right back to her and tell her it's wrong to steal. And ... in the future, I'd be careful about what friends I chose."

Monica thought about that a moment. She looked at Carrie in wonder. "You're something else, Carrie. I mean you're really something else. You're always so sure what's right. You never get into trouble and you're never ... confused." She studied Carrie thoughtfully. "How do you do it?"

"Well, I can't say that I'm never confused, but I think it's because I was raised as a Bahá'í."

"I know you're a Bahá'í, you already told me. But is that it? It's because you're a Bahá'í?"

"I think so, Monica."

"And your parents taught you this ... this religion?"

"Yes, for as long as I can remember."

Monica pondered this for a while. Then she said in a halting voice, "Well, I think you're lucky. I think you're lucky to have parents you can talk to – who take the time to teach you to be ... to be so sure of yourself."

Carrie met Monica's gaze. In those eyes she saw such a need for love, assurance and faith – something she herself had always had. And very softly she said, almost to herself, "Yes, Monica, I guess I am."

PLAY IT RIGHT

Bobby tried again, his chubby face red with the effort and his damp blond hair plastered to his head. Turning to the girl playing 'Zaynab', he said in deep tones, "We are called upon to defend our lives against a treacherous assailant, and not to wage holy war against him."

"That's fine, Bobby. That's enough for today," said Mrs. Henderson, his Bahá'í Sunday School teacher. "I think you'll all be ready in time for the children's conference. We should know the date soon, in fact the LSA is discussing it tonight. But," she turned to Pam, "you'll have to work a little more on your lines."

Pam, who was playing the part of Zaynab in their play called *Zanján!* answered, "All right, I'll practice my lines over the weekend."

Bobby picked up his script and started for the door but stopped when he noticed Megan sitting alone in the corner of the room.

"Hey Megan, are you coming to softball this afternoon?" he asked.

"Yeah, I guess so," she answered, her chestnut hair hiding her freckled face. Bobby peered down at her.

"What's the matter? You look so glum these days."

"Nothing much," she said, looking down at her feet.

A for Effort

"Do you like the play? I mean, do you think we'll be okay in front of all those kids?"

"Oh," she said, looking up, "I think you're great!" She stopped a moment and then blurted out, "I just wish I could get up there and act like that."

"But why can't you? Mrs. Henderson wanted to give you the part of Zaynab first. Why'd you say no?"

"I could never do it. You know me . . . up in front of all those people . . . I can't even raise my hand in class."

"You should have at least *tried*." Bobby couldn't understand this. Acting was something he really liked. In fact he had a leading role in his school play too. But his part as Ḥujjat was his favorite. He had worked hard on his lines and almost knew them perfectly.

The Local Spiritual Assembly was planning a mini children's conference and inviting all the Bahá'í kids from communities around the city. Bobby and his Bahá'í class would be presenting their play *Zanján!*.

"It's no use," replied Megan, "I'm just no good . . . I can't do anything right."

"You just gotta try, Megan – you can't do anything if you don't try."

Megan didn't answer, she just lowered her head again. Bobby got up. "See you at softball."

"Okay."

That night Bobby was still up doing his homework when his parents came home from the LSA meeting. His older sister Jenny had finished hers and gone to bed.

"You're up late, you should have finished that a long time ago," his mother said as she hung up her coat.

"I was studying my lines for *Zanján!* and then I remembered I had homework in science."

"Now Bobby, you know your homework always comes first." She smiled. "I guess this play means a lot to you, doesn't it? You've worked so hard on it."

"Yeah," said Bobby. And it did. He had always loved the story about Zaynab and how she had dressed as a man to join Ḥujjat and the other Bábís defending the fort in Zanján. Somehow when he repeated the lines spoken by Ḥujjat over a hundred years ago, he felt different, almost like he himself were a hero.

"By the way, Bobby, the LSA chose a date for the conference. It's going to be all day on Saturday, January 28th."

Bobby looked up from his homework in horror. "But Mom, that's the day of our school play! We'll be rehearsing *all* day! Morning and afternoon!"

Bobby's mom frowned. "I'm sorry, Bobby, I forgot all about it. But anyway, sweetheart, I'm sure that's the only date we can do it. I think the LSA has something planned for all the other weekends in January, and February too." She paused. "We'll check it out. Maybe we can find another time. I'll ask at the LSA meeting next Tuesday."

Bobby was worried. He finished his homework but his mind was only half on it. As he slipped into bed he comforted himself. The LSA wouldn't do this to him. They'd find a way to change the date.

Next Tuesday Bobby was waiting up when his parents came home.

"Up again, Bobby? This is getting to be a bad habit," his father said. "I told Jenny to make sure you got to bed at a decent time. You didn't forget your homework again, I hope?"

"No, Dad," replied Bobby sheepishly. "Jenny told me to go up but I thought, well, maybe the LSA had changed the date of the children's conference. I've just gotta know!"

Bobby's dad sat down beside him at the dining-room table. "Bobby," he said gently, "the LSA really couldn't find a way. We talked for some time about it – January 28th is the best day for everyone."

"But not for me! I can't miss rehearsal for the school play, Dad. I've got the lead part. They're counting on me."

"I know, Bobby. Your mom and I talked about it on the way home. You'll have to miss the children's conference."

"But who's going to play Ḥujjat?"

"We talked about that too," said his mother. "Mrs. Henderson thinks it's a good chance to let Megan try something."

"But she's a girl! She can't play Ḥujjat!"

"She'll be dressed up in a turban."

"But Megan's much too scared to get up in front of people. She wouldn't even play Zaynab!"

"When she sees there's no one else to do it, I'm sure she'll accept. The LSA thought it might be a good idea if you helped her learn her lines."

Bobby couldn't believe it. "But I've worked harder than anyone else! They can't do this to me!" He got up and walked to the window, kicking an armchair on the way. Then he turned.

"If the LSA really cared, they'd find another day." He dropped into the armchair and crossed his arms defiantly.

Bobby's parents looked at each other. His father

got up and took a seat beside him while his mother settled on the couch.

"The LSA really did try to find a solution, Bobby. They care about you and about everyone else too. Anyway, Bobby, whatever the LSA decides, we should try very hard to respect their decision. Sometimes things just don't work out the way we would like."

"It would work out if they tried."

Bobby's dad thought for a moment, then he said, "Bobby, what would you do if Bahá'u'lláh Himself set the date for this children's conference? Would you be angry? Would you argue?"

Bobby considered that. "No . . . No one can argue with Bahá'u'lláh, Dad, you know that. But the LSA isn't Bahá'u'lláh!"

"Ah, maybe not, but Bahá'u'lláh Himself created the Local Spiritual Assembly. Look, do you remember when we talked about what 'infallible' means?"

"Yeah, sure. It means whoever's infallible can't make mistakes. And you yourself said the LSA is not infallible – so it can make mistakes."

"Hold your horses, darling. Let me finish. Anyway, the Báb, Bahá'u'lláh, 'Abdu'l-Bahá, Shoghi Effendi and now the Universal House of Justice are all infallible. That means they are protected by God and can't make mistakes. No matter what they say, we obey them without question."

"Yeah . . ."

"But the Local Spiritual Assembly is not infallible and can sometimes make mistakes."

"That's what I was saying."

"But it doesn't mean we don't obey them and respect everything they say. As I said, Bahá'u'lláh created the LSA Himself, so that we could have order in the world. And what a wonderful new world order it will be when we Bahá'ís work together in unity. Now, to work in unity we all have to work in one direction. The LSA sets the direction in our community. If we all work in different directions, we'll never get anything done. So, even if the LSA makes a decision we think isn't right, we still obey it." He paused, "Let's say the LSA decides to teach the Faith in a certain way and everybody obeys even if they don't agree. If the decision really isn't good and everybody is trying to make it work, well, we'll see right away if it works or not and the LSA can change it if they have to."

"But," Mom added, "if nobody tries to make it work, we'll never know whether it's a good decision or not."

"At the same time," Dad continued, "a decision can be wrong, but if everybody obeys it with a good loving spirit, why, God can make everything work out well in the end anyway. It's the spirit that counts, can you see that?"

"Yeah, I guess so. You mean we have to work together."

"That's right, that's why Bahá'u'lláh came. To teach us to make our hearts so loving that we're always unified, always following a common purpose.

"It's true, Bobby, that if we don't agree with the LSA we can always explain why nicely and ask them to think about it again, like you asked them to try and change the date of the children's conference. But once you do that and they make a decision – well, you just have to respect it. You do your best to make it work."

"Like helping Megan learn her lines," Bobby said glumly.

His mother came up and sat on the arm of his

chair, putting her arm around his shoulders. "Yes, like helping Megan learn her lines even if you would rather play that part with all your heart." She paused. "You know," she said, tapping his head with her finger, "something good always happens when we obey our LSA, just you wait and see. There's a reason for everything."

"All right, I'll do it." Bobby finally managed a grudging smile. "But," he muttered almost to himself, "a *girl* playing Ḥujjat? And Megan?" He sighed.

His father winked at his mother and grinned. "Time for bed, super star, get going."

Bobby tramped off to bed, thinking it was going to be a long three weeks before the play.

"I just can't, Bobby. Really, I'm too stupid to learn even half of these lines."

"Aw Megan, you just *think* you're stupid. You always say you can't do this, you think you can't do that . . . Give it a try. You're a lot smarter than most girls I know."

"Is that a compliment?"

"Well, you can catch, can't you?"

"Sure, but . . ."

"Keep trying then!"

"Okay!"

Bobby sighed as he thought about what his mother had said. Something good may come of it – there's a reason for everything . . . He couldn't imagine a reason for *this* as he watched Megan frowning with concentration as she looked at her script.

Two hours later, a very tired Megan stood up again, her hands outstretched, her head thrown back, "Never shall I be willing to barter, for all the

A for Effort

treasures and honors this world can give me, the undying loyalty I bear His Cause..."

"That's great!" Bobby exclaimed. "You're better than I ever thought you could be!" And she was. Once she got into her lines, Megan seemed to have a new confidence. It's almost like she's not Megan any more, Bobby thought. Like pretending to be someone else makes her more sure of herself.

Megan stood there, her face flushed with pleasure. "Maybe I *can* do it, Bobby. Maybe I can!"

"And maybe even better than I can," said Bobby thoughtfully.

The next three weeks were busy ones for Bobby, balancing rehearsals for his school play, coaching Megan and keeping up with his homework – which his father insisted must come first. He was still disappointed about losing his part as Ḥujjat in the Baháʼí play, but at the same time he was proud that Megan was doing so well.

Finally, the night before the children's conference and the school play arrived. He was helping his mother wrap small bags of candy for the children when the phone rang.

"It's for you, Bobby," called his father. "I think it's Mr Barnfield."

Bobby went to the phone, wondering what Mr. Barnfield, the science teacher who was directing the school play, would want. He picked up the phone.

"Hello."

"Hello, Bobby, Mr. Barnfield here."

"Oh, hello, Mr. Barnfield."

"I'm calling about tomorrow's rehearsal. I know that you kids have been working pretty hard and since you've done such a good job, maybe we can

Play it Right

skip rehearsal tomorrow morning. You know, just rehearse in the afternoon. Some of the other teachers and I thought a whole day at it would just tire you out."

"That's great, Mr. Barnfield. I mean... that sounds like a good idea."

"Okay, tomorrow at 2:00 sharp."

"Okay!"

He hung up, but then instead of running to his parents with the good news he stood for a moment deep in thought. Finally, his father asked, "So, what did he want?"

Bobby approached the table where his mother and father were still bagging the candy. "He says we won't have a rehearsal tomorrow morning."

His mother looked up, "Why that's wonderful news, Bobby. You can play the part of Ḥujjat after all. The play's on in the morning, isn't it?"

Bobby sunk down on to a dining-room chair. "Yeah."

"You don't look too happy about it."

"That's... that's because I can't. Megan's been working so hard on the part. I couldn't just go in and take it away from her now."

"No," his mother said quietly, "I guess you can't. I didn't think about that."

Bobby sighed. Then slowly he began to smile. "But I *can* go watch her."

His father came over and put a hand on his shoulder. "That you can, son." He looked down at Bobby, pride written all over his face.

The next morning Bobby didn't appear at the children's conference until the play was about to begin. His parents had been kept busy with their part of the preparations at home. Bobby was glad. He wanted to surprise Megan.

So it wasn't until Megan came out on stage to deliver her first lines that she saw Bobby in the front row. Her eyes widened in surprise and then she grinned. Bobby grinned back and gave her the thumbs up sign.

Megan did very well once she got into the swing of it. Bobby could see that she was nervous at first, stumbling over her first few lines. She glanced at him and he gave her his most encouraging "You can do it!" look. Once she gathered her courage, she didn't look back at him once.

As the play moved to its close, Megan, wrapped in her eastern robes, her chestnut hair covered with a turban, was kneeling. Her voice trembled as she spoke the last words of Ḥujjat on earth, "Would that a myriad of lives were mine, would that I possessed the riches of the whole earth and its glory, that I might resign them all freely and joyously in Thy path."

There was a moment's silence followed by a tremendous burst of applause and soon Megan, still kneeling, found herself surrounded by both children and parents who came on stage to congratulate her. Bobby held back until the crowd had cleared. When he finally came up, Mrs. Henderson had her arm around Megan.

"I *knew* you could do it, Megan," Mrs. Henderson told her, hugging her more closely.

"*I* didn't," said Megan, "until Bobby bullied me into it." She threw him a grateful glance.

Bobby just smiled. He remembered his mother's words, "You know, something good always happens when we obey the LSA. Just you wait and see. There's a reason for everything."

Bobby suddenly understood what that reason was as he saw Megan's eyes shining with joy and pride. She really had become a new person and all because they had pulled together to make the LSA decision work.

BEYOND ALL THAT

I don't much like getting up in front of a bunch of people, much less speaking. But there was nothing for it, because when Mr. Kenrick speaks, you obey. He was chairman of our Local Spiritual Assembly. Not that he was bossy or anything, but he had this air of authority that made you straighten up. Anyway he'd already called me and everybody was looking at me.

I got up. "Well, we ... er ... we've started this coffee house on Saturday nights here at the Bahá'í Center, as you know. And it's going pretty well — lots of kids come. We had seventy-four last Saturday night. We, uh, drink tea, coffee and sit around and talk, and some kids bring musical instruments and all that. Uh ... oh, and one Saturday night a month we start the coffee house evening off with a fireside."

I sat down with relief. Everyone applauded and Mr. Kenrick got up again and said what a nice job we were doing and that several "young people" were already interested in the Faith because of it. That made me feel good because we'd tried so hard to get it going.

That's why I was surprised when Mr. Eberhart stood up looking so grim. I mean, he always looks grim, but that night he looked grimmer than usual, and besides that he had some papers in his hand that he seemed determined to read from, *and* he was looking straight at me!

I mean, Mr. Eberhart's okay. He's been a Bahá'í for years and years – in fact I heard somewhere that he was the first Bahá'í in our city. But somehow I always got the idea that he didn't approve of me. I kinda tried to stay out of his way. Unfortunately, that night I seemed to be directly in his path.

"Dear friends," he began, "I take the occasion of this sacred and blessèd Feast" – he always talked like that, but we didn't mind; we were used to it – "to bring your attention to what I feel is a serious matter. I would like to read to you from a text I have brought with me." He rattled his papers, cleared his throat, adjusted his glasses and continued: "Our beloved Guardian Shoghi Effendi says that a chaste and holy life – and here I read, 'with its implications of modesty, purity, temperance, decency, and clean-mindedness, involves no less . . .' he stopped there, looked around and repeated, '*no less* than the exercise of *moderation* in all that pertains to *dress, language, amusements*, and *all artistic and literary avocations*.' *Advent of Divine Justice*, page 24." At that he removed his glasses with a flourish, looked at me pointedly and sat down.

Well, I thought that over for a minute but I really didn't know what to think and I'm sure no one else did either because they all looked equally bewildered. I took a sneak peek at the clothes I was wearing that night, but they checked out. My newest jeans and a freshly ironed yellow, striped shirt. My tennis shoes might have been a little dirty . . .

Mr. Kenrick, forever an example of tact and good

manners, politely asked, "Jack, perhaps you could explain yourself a bit further."

"I thought it was entirely clear, but then perhaps not everyone knows what goes on at these coffee house evenings . . ." I cringed. "You see, I happened to stroll in the other night and frankly I was shocked at what I saw and heard. First of all, everyone was sitting on the floor. There are perfectly good chairs in this Center that we paid good money for, but no, they had to sit on the floor. Then, I noticed that these young kids weren't even discussing religion – anything but! I thought the purpose of these gatherings was to teach the Faith.

"Thirdly, I noticed this gathering had attracted undesirable elements of the community – what I think you call 'punk' these days – yellow hair, pink hair, all sticking up in all directions, outrageous clothing." *That's Agatha*, I thought, she was even getting pretty interested in the Faith. "That does not seem to me to represent moderation in dress!

"Fourth and last of all, I happened to sit down and listen to some of the music. I couldn't believe my ears – it was filthy and vile!" Oh no, I thought to myself miserably, he must have walked in when Chad was playing. I had to admit he had a point there . . . "I propose that the Local Spiritual Assembly take matters firmly in hand and provide more regulated, *clean-minded* activities for our youth. I propose that the coffee house be disbanded and substituted with youth firesides."

I felt my heart sink. Our precious coffee house! Now, you know how I feel about speaking, but when I really get a bee in my bonnet . . .

First I tried to control myself; this was Feast after

all. I raised my hand. Mr. Kenrick, looking distinctly wary, nodded to me.

"Mr. Eberhart," I began courteously, "I know our coffee house may be hard to understand as a teaching activity, but let me try to explain. We want to attract youth to the Center by giving them a place to go to and relax on Saturday nights. Now, while they are here, we Bahá'í youth try to teach them the Faith little by little. But we don't talk about the Faith *all* the time – that would just scare people away. It's not a Bahá'í meeting."

"And do you think our Center should be open to non-Bahá'í activities?" he responded.

"It's a public service!" I shot out.

"The secretary will make note of this question for the Local Spiritual Assembly," Mr. Kenrick said diplomatically.

"At the same time," I continued, as courteously as possible, but I was getting a little heated up, "our Center should be open to everyone and we should try to teach everyone. Most of us Bahá'í kids don't wear punk styles, but that doesn't mean all kids who do are bad or that we shouldn't teach them."

"It gives the Bahá'í Center a bad reputation," grumbled Mr. Eberhart.

"As long as the youth are not indecent we can't judge!" I shot back.

Now, I *knew* that Bahá'ís shouldn't get into arguments that cause disunity. I knew, really knew, from deepenings and reading the writings that if anything made 'Abdu'l-Bahá sad it was for Bahá'ís to argue. And I really didn't want to make 'Abdu'l-Bahá sad. But I was a little confused here about the difference between "consulting frankly" and arguing. I decided maybe I'd try to make peace.

"Mr. Eberhart, you were right about one thing. We should never have let Chad sing. But believe me he was the only one who sang like that. It won't happen again," I said contritely, and I meant it.

"Maybe it won't happen again because you won't have your coffee house again!"

"Oh no!" I wailed, and the words had come out on their own.

Mr. Kenrick thankfully jumped in at this point. "I'm sure the secretary has this all noted down for the next LSA meeting. Now perhaps we can hear our treasurer's report..."

Next LSA meeting... I wanted to go and make sure they got the story straight, but Mr. Kenrick assured me that several members had visited the coffee house and would know the details. So I just had to sit and wait. It was hard but finally, at the next Bahá'í meeting, Mr. Kenrick came up to me before it started.

"Alex," he said, "the LSA discussed the Saturday night coffee house gatherings and asked me to talk to you and the other members of your coffee house committee."

"Yes?" I said, holding my breath.

He smiled, "There's no problem, you can continue."

I let my breath out. We'd won.

"But," he said, "The LSA would like one of the youth to be in charge of who plays and sings there. It should be organized so that there are no unseemly or vulgar lyrics sung."

"Yes, Mr. Kenrick." I guess my grin must have been wide enough to stick my foot in.

Mr. Kenrick paused, "You know, Alex, I know you're happy and perhaps, just a little, you might think you've 'won'. But in this Faith nobody wins until there is complete unity."

I felt my grin slip a little. Somehow it didn't feel so good anymore. "Yes, Mr. Kenrick."

He continued, "You know, Mr. Eberhart is a very devoted Bahá'í and he's served the Faith selflessly for many years. If sometimes he's difficult to get along with, it's because he loves the Faith so much and he wishes to protect it. He was a Bahá'í youth once too, and sometimes it's difficult for him to accept the fact that the Bahá'í youth of today are different from in his day."

"Yes, Mr. Kenrick, thanks, I understand." And maybe I did just a little. I turned to enter the meeting hall.

"Alex," he said again before I'd taken a step, "when I say unity, I mean true unity, true love and understanding. It's just a suggestion, but maybe you'll need to find some way to make it up with Mr. Eberhart. Just staying out of someone's way doesn't mean true unity."

I stopped at that. Had he read my thoughts or what? Because that's exactly what was at the back of my mind. I had thought the best way to avoid *disunity* would be to stay out of his way.

Mr. Kenrick left me then, but I continued to stand in the doorway. As I thought about it I realized that maybe just avoiding disunity wasn't the way. True unity was another thing altogether. I shook my head. I couldn't imagine myself talking and laughing with Mr. Eberhart – why, he hardly ever smiled. Or was that true? I thought back. He did laugh and smile sometimes, just not with me. But, I thought with a sudden burst of anger, that's his fault, not mine.

He's a long-term Bahá'í; he should know more about promoting unity than I do.

That didn't feel right either. Like Mr. Kenrick said, it was hard for Mr. Eberhart. I left the doorway determined to somehow make friends. I guess he was still sore about the coffee house and I soon realized that my cheerful attempts to greet him must sound like I was gloating. All I got back were a few sour grunts. It's difficult for him, I kept saying to myself, but it wasn't easy for me...

I went home thoughtful and depressed. All that week I mulled over the problem. I had sincerely decided to make friends with Mr. Eberhart, but every time I called him to mind I quailed. I'd push that negative thought of him out of my mind and imagine a smiling, kind Mr. Eberhart. *That* thought kept dissolving in thin air and I'd have to shove it back into place. It wasn't easy...

It wasn't until next Saturday night when we were trying to decide on a speaker for the next coffee house fireside that I hit on a plan. We would invite Mr. Eberhart to speak – a show of goodwill. No, not a *show*, I corrected myself. He wasn't a bad speaker and I knew that if I were really serious about unity, true unity, I would have to be sincere.

I thought uneasily about Agatha. It wasn't like we had the place filled with punk types, that was kind of out now anyway – but there *was* Agatha and she was sure to be there. I never knew what color her hair would be next. She was a real character. As a matter of principle she refused to speak to anyone over twenty if she could help it. But slowly she was becoming serious about the Faith. She had a lot of good qualities behind her rebel front.

The next day at the deepening, I summoned up all

my sincerity. I knew I'd need it. I approached Mr. Eberhart at the coffee urn.

"Mr. Eberhart," I began, trying not to sound too cheerful this time.

Grunt.

"I was, I mean we were wondering if maybe you could, I mean, if you don't mind . . ." here I took a deep breath and rushed on, "if you could speak at our coffee house fireside this Saturday night."

There I'd done it. I waited.

He just looked at me. I waited some more. I guess it began to sink in because he almost dropped his coffee cup.

"I mean," I continued – I'd thought this out carefully – "I mean, it might be good for the kids. You've been a Bahá'í so long, we . . . we need someone like you." And I meant it; it wasn't so important that I'd said it, it was important that I meant it.

Well, once he'd got hold of his coffee cup, Mr. Eberhart just stood there looking at me. He didn't move a muscle – just looked at me. I began to wonder if I'd put the poor man into shock. Then suddenly, as if it were the most natural thing in the world, he said, "I'd be glad to, Alex."

I sighed with relief. No smile, no instant friendship, but he'd accepted.

I was a bit nervous that Saturday night. I'd gathered every chair in the Center into the meeting hall, even pinching the secretary's chair so that even if someone wanted to sit on the floor, they couldn't – there wasn't an inch of space.

The room filled up. I stopped counting at sixty-five and at 7:30 sharp, in walked Mr. Eberhart, punctual as usual. I'd been just a little afraid he'd bring along all those quotations from Shoghi Effendi, but his hands were free of papers.

He began to speak. Now, I'd heard Mr. Eberhart speak before with all those big words and fine sounding phrases and I wondered how it would go over. The youth needed his knowledge and experience, but I was worried it might not come across.

But that night, as he faced us, it was like he dropped all that, just for us. He spoke simply and humbly and it was as if he was trying to get through to us on our own terms. Suddenly I knew that something had happened at that coffee urn. Like I said, there had been no smile, no instant friendship, but something had happened and we were seeing the results.

He stopped speaking as abruptly as he had started, shuffled his feet around, adjusted his glasses and then said in conclusion, "I know you kids might find it hard to understand an old man; there are so many years and different experiences between us, but these teachings, the teachings of a new Manifestation of God on earth, coming only once in a thousand years, go beyond all that. And, if we can just look beyond it, to the things that really matter, why," and here he smiled, "we can do wonders together."

In the silence that followed I was suddenly worried that somehow his words hadn't gotten through, that maybe I was the only one who felt his words so deeply. But I was wrong because at that instant came a sudden thunderous burst of applause. Mr. Eberhart had brought the house down.

It took him by surprise. He stood there, blinking and looking slightly bewildered, but I could see he was pleased.

When the applause died down, up stood Agatha.

Her hair was purple and green this time – she'd outdone herself.

So much for a perfect evening, I groaned inwardly.

She spoke. "I just wanted to say," she paused until all the applause had stopped and there was perfect silence. "I just wanted to say that up until this evening I wasn't so sure about this Bahá'í business. I mean, one day I'd be sure, and the next, well, I'd wonder how I could get along with some of these older types – or how they'd get along with me. Maybe they wouldn't accept me, I'd say to myself. But tonight I realized, just like Mr. Eberhart said, that these..these differences," she patted her hair, grinned, and everyone else did too, "just don't matter. Like he said, the Manifestation of God goes beyond all that. So, I'd like to say that as of right now I'm a Bahá'í." She paused and then continued with a new found humility that didn't sound in the least like Agatha, "I just hope I'm worthy."

With that she sat down and smiled disarmingly at Mr. Eberhart, her purple and green hair shimmering in the spotlight she'd chosen to sit under.

Poor Mr. Eberhart. He didn't know whether to be happy or aghast. During the question period that followed, he'd smile one moment and look totally dismayed another.

Three other youth became Bahá'ís that night and I'll have to say that the next Feast after that was sure interesting. After all, Agatha and the new youth were his babies, he'd brought them into the Faith, and to his embarrassment everyone knew it.

But it wasn't so bad in the end. He became quite used to Agatha plunking down beside him from time to time and she'd listen, with those wide eyes of hers, to one ponderous discourse or another of his. After a while she even let her hair grow back to its natural color. "Too much trouble to keep it up," she said, "too busy, what with being a Bahá'í and everything."

And Mr. Eberhart and me? Well, I won't say we didn't have our difficult moments, but then there *are* things that go beyond all that.

FOUR SIMPLE WORDS

"How many eggs, Mom?" Ben called out as he stood before the refrigerator door.

"Six."

Ben carefully drew out six eggs and laid them on the table in the middle of the kitchen. "And how much butter?"

"514 grams."

Ben stamped his foot in exasperation. "Oh, come on, Mom!"

"Figure it out, honey. It's not difficult."

"Oh, all right!" Ben pressed his dark curly head against the refrigerator door and muttered his calculations aloud. Finally he announced, "Approximately one pound, two ounces."

"Very good, you're getting better!" Mom chuckled as she pulled the canister of flour down from the shelf.

"Yeah, sure," said Ben. He took the required amount of butter out of the refrigerator and put that on the table too.

"That's a lot of butter," he remarked. "I thought you didn't eat butter. Your diet and all."

Mom blushed a little. "Well, I *have* been fasting for nineteen days. I suppose it won't hurt. Anyway it will be Naw-Rúz in . . ." she looked at her watch, "exactly 8½ hours. Moms can celebrate too, you know."

The telephone rang and she went to answer it while Ben mulled over the cook book.

"Sure Betty, I'd be glad to . . ."

"Uh huh . . ."

"By the way, Betty, we're having a celebration here tonight. I wonder if you and Bob would like to come. You can bring the children."

"Yes, a Bahá'í celebration."

"What's the Bahá'í Faith? Well . . ."

There she goes again, thought Ben as he watched his mother's face light up at that magic question, "What's the Bahá'í Faith?" We'll *never* get these cookies made now! Mom was always teaching.

"Sure, Betty. Anyway, I've got to go now. I'm making cookies with Ben. I'll explain more tonight if we get the chance . . . Fine, see you."

Mom hung up and came back to the kitchen table, peering over Ben's shoulder at the cook book. "Let's see, six cups of flour." she handed Ben the cup measure.

"That was Mrs. Rogers?" he asked as he carefully measured the flour and poured it into a big blue bowl.

"Yes."

"I thought you'd already taught the Faith to all your friends."

"Well, I've been a bit careful with Betty. I know she doesn't believe in God so I've been looking for the right moment to bring it up. Thought our Naw-Rúz party was perfect." She paused. "Have you invited anyone, Ben?"

He knew she'd get around to asking that question. Well, he hadn't. "No."

"Oh."

He could hear the disappointment in her voice and it cut him. He burst out, "It's easy for *you*. But maybe it's not so easy for everyone else!"

"What's so easy?" asked Mom, surprised.

"Teaching the Faith. You know everything. When someone asks you a question, you know all the answers. If someone asks *me* a question I just sit there like a dumb bunny. I don't know what to say. I don't know enough to teach!"

Mom thought about that as she went to the refrigerator to get the milk. She paused as she set it next to the blue bowl. "I guess you're right. It's not easy in the beginning. But the way I see it, Ben, is that no one can learn to teach if they don't start doing it. That's how I learned to teach. People always asked me questions at the beginning that I didn't know. But when that happened I just said I didn't know. Afterwards I'd go look the question up or I'd ask another Bahá'í. Then the next time someone asked me, I'd know the answer."

"It's easy for you, grown-ups don't make fun of people. If I told my friends I was a Bahá'í, why they'd just make fun of me."

"I don't know about that. And I mean, it's not always easy for me. Some people stop talking to me when they learn I'm a Bahá'í."

"They do?"

"It's happened. But I try not to mind. I just try to be as friendly as I can. And I never teach people who show they're not interested. Anyway, you'd be surprised how many people are interested, even children."

Ben pulled a bag of sugar out of the canister.

"Okay," Mom said, "one cup of white sugar, two cups of brown sugar."

Ben measured out the sugar and poured it into a white bowl his mother brought to him. "But why can't we teach by just being good Bahá'ís? I remember in the last Feast you read something about how when a Bahá'í goes into a town, why, everyone should just know he's a Bahá'í by the way he acts. I'm a good Bahá'í aren't I?"

Mom stopped at that, her clear grey eyes glowing with pleasure. She reached over and ruffled Ben's hair. "Sweetheart, just the fact that you're listening in Feast and thinking about what you hear shows what a good Bahá'í you're becoming. But," she said slowly, "people may see we're different but how are they going to know why if we don't tell them? How are they going to know that Bahá'u'lláh has come?" She walked around the table and took Ben's hands in her own. "We hold in our hands the only way that the people of the world are going to know peace. People are hungry because the world doesn't know about Bahá'u'lláh. Children just like you die in wars everyday just because we haven't taken the name of Bahá'u'lláh to them. We hold the key to all the problems of the world and we can't keep it to ourselves." She looked deeply into his eyes, "We just *can't*."

Then she smiled, "But you don't have to go out and tell everyone you know all on the same day! You just have to look for opportunities to teach. Something will come up – just you wait and see. And before long you'll see ways to teach all the time. Just take your time now."

When the cookies were done and neatly stacked on three separate plates, Ben asked permission to go play. No sooner was it given than he grabbed a few cookies and ran down the back steps of his apartment building. Hank, the custodian of the building, had promised to show him how to make a toy airplane out of plywood. Hank was a big man and Ben could see him sitting on the bottom step from three flights up by peering down through the railings. He tiptoed down the last flight and meant to surprise Hank but just as Ben was about to touch him, Hank said, "I hear you, don't try it, son."

Ben flopped down beside him. "How is it you *always* hear me?" he asked as he handed Hank a cookie.

"Thanks Ben. Well, if you tear down the first two flights, it's kinda hard *not* to hear you!"

"Oh yeah, I guess you would, huh? Can we make the airplane today like you said?"

"I'm real sorry, Ben. I just didn't have time to go round and pick up the wood last night." He laid a grizzled black hand covered with coarse white hair on Ben's shoulder. "We'll do it tomorrow for sure."

"Okay," said Ben, trying to hide his disappointment.

"Now don't go saying 'okay' like it's the end of the world. I just had some problems last night and didn't get to it."

Ben looked at the enormous form beside him in blue overalls and wondered what kind of problems Hank could have. He wondered if they could be problems like the ones his mother talked about sometimes.

"You got problems, Hank? Anything I can help you with?"

Hank turned around slowly and studied Ben. "Now just what are you doing worrying about my problems, son?"

Ben lowered his head ashamed. "Just thought maybe I could help you, Hank. I didn't mean to be nosy."

A for Effort

"No, I guess you didn't." Hank turned back around and studied his paint splattered shoes. "But that's just it, Ben, you *think*. You think about other people, you think about me – always bringing me cookies and things. You're different, now why are you so different?"

There it was. Plain as can be. A chance to teach, just like Mom said. Now all he had to do was get the words out, "Because I'm a Bahá'í." Four simple words.

"I gotta go, Hank." Wrong four words.

"But you just *got* here!"

"Yeah, but I gotta go." And with that Ben dashed up the stairs. Why couldn't he get those four words out? After the first flight he slowed down, trying to work it out. He started pulling himself up the stairs slowly, his hands on both rails. Ben looked down at his hands. Two hands splattered with the cookie dough he had forgotten to wash off. What was it that Mom had said about his hands? "We hold in our hands the only way . . ." Her words seemed to echo off the walls. "People are hungry, Ben, because the world doesn't know about Bahá'u'lláh." Maybe Hank's kids were hungry, maybe that was his problem.

In one instant Ben had turned around and dashed down the stairs again. He plopped down beside Hank, who had taken out his lunch.

"You back already?"

"Yeah."

"Want some of this sandwich?"

"No."

Hank bit into his sandwich. "Good sandwich, sure you don't want some?"

"I'm a Bahá'í."

"What?"

"I'm a Bahá'í. That's why I'm different. Because I'm a Bahá'í."

"Oh." Hank looked amused. "What's a Bahá'í?"

Now it's true that Ben had gotten his four words out, but he hadn't thought too much about what he was going to say next.

"A Bahá'í is a . . . a person."

"Oh." Hank thought about that. "What's a Bahá'í person?"

"It's someone who believes in Bahá'u'lláh."

"What's Bahá'u'lláh?"

'Well, He's a man, a Prophet really. He's going to bring all the people of the world together so we'll have just one religion . . . and . . . and people won't be hungry." At that he took a quick glance at Hank.

"Where's He live?"

"He doesn't live anywhere . . . I mean, He's dead."

"So how's He gonna bring all the people of the world together if He's dead?"

Hank had a point there. Now how could he explain that? Ben buried his face in his hands to think that out. Then he sat up straight. "You see, He left us a bunch of books. Now we read these books and these *books* are going to bring us together."

Hank tapped his moustache thoughtfully. "Books . . . kinda like the Bible, right?"

Ben sighed with relief. "Right!" He stood up. "Anyway, we're having a party at my house tonight. It's a New Year's party."

"New Year's? In March?"

"Yeah, wanna come?"

"Well, I don't know, Ben. I gotta lot to do . . ."

"There'll be *lots* of cookies . . ."

A for Effort

Hank looked at Ben's hopeful face. He smiled. "Well, in *that* case . . . I guess I will!"

"Great! I'll go tell my mom." Ben started up the stairs. Hank stood up.

"Whoa down, I'm coming with you. Your mother wanted me to look at that leaky sink faucet."

Mom was setting the table for Ben's lunch when they walked in.

"Come to see about that leaky faucet."

"Oh sure, Hank, just a minute."

Hank looked around the room at the prepared food piled up on every surface, including the three plates of cookies. "Looks like you've got enough to feed an army!"

"That's right, Hank. We're having a party tonight. And I was just going to ask you if you'd like to come."

"I think Ben beat you to it."

Mom looked surprised. "He did?"

"Yeah, told me all about it. How you're Bahá'í people and believe in Bahá'lláh."

"Bahá'u'lláh," corrected Ben.

"Yeah, Bahá'u'lláh, and about how He's dead and wrote a lot of books."

"He told you all that?"

"Sure did, right on the back stairs." Then with a wink he added, "He also said you'd have *lots* of cookies, and I couldn't pass *that* up, now – could I?"

Mom smiled what must have been the biggest smile Ben had ever seen. She pulled Ben over next to her and gave him a big hug. "No," she said, "I guess you couldn't."

SUNDAY'S FIRE

The first time I saw Sunday's fire was when his wife Sarah was scraping cow stomach. We had just arrived at the National Bahá'í Center but instead of going in the front door Mom and Dad hurried around the back. My sister and I followed and before we knew it we were laughingly gathered up into strong, warm, black arms. I was surprised and a little afraid. I mean, I didn't really know whose arms they were. Finally, I plucked up my courage and peered into the blackest, flashingest eyes you can imagine.

"So, little blue eyes, what's your name?"

"Uh . . . Marie . . . Sir."

"And little green eyes?"

"That's my sister, Elizabeth."

"Well, Marie and Elizabeth, you sit here." And before we knew it we were deposited on two tiny stools before a little wood fire and left to ourselves while Mom and Dad, "Big Black Eyes" (they called him Sunday) and his wife embraced and kissed and patted each other on the back and said things like "Such a long time!"

While I was contemplating the fire and wondering why in the world anyone would be named Sunday, I didn't notice that Sarah was back on another stool on the other side of the fire. Soon her scraping and

A for Effort

splashing noises in an enormous enamel tub drew my attention.

Little Elizabeth was interested too and went over to investigate. Her eyes grew big and I could tell her small hand was itching to touch what was inside the tub.

It strayed closer and closer until, smack! Sarah's knife came crashing down on the board she was scraping inside the tub. Alarmed, we both looked up at her grinning face.

"You no touch . . . dirty!"

Elizabeth was convinced and didn't "touch", but I inched my stool over to get a look. Sarah was back to work scraping what looked like webbed flesh covered with green slime. The board, the water and the tub were all covered with green slime.

"Cow stomach," Sarah announced.

Cow stomach. I mulled this over and then pointing at it and hoping to correctly imitate her telegraphic English asked, "You eat?"

"Oh no! Cook first, *after* chop."

Being a bit relieved but still confused I laughed, "You no eat, only chop."

Sarah stopped and studied me a minute.

"Chop is eat," she said, obviously wondering if I were just big for my age to have such a limited vocabulary.

"Ah! Chop is eat!" I corrected myself, having just completed my first lesson in pidgin English.

Sarah and Sunday were from Nigeria and were now guardians of the National Bahá'í Center in our French African country. I soon learned Sarah hardly even spoke Pidgin English and usually spoke a mixture of Pidgin, French and Ibo. The French didn't bother me, because my sister and I had been born in

French Africa, but the Ibo left me rather bewildered until my blank look convinced Sarah that she'd better find another word.

She often wasn't successful at finding the right word but we got along famously anyway and Elizabeth and I were soon quite at home. Sunday, having been to school, spoke English as we knew it and could intervene in emergencies.

Maybe you're wondering why this story is called Sunday's Fire. Well, it's hard to say because nothing really happened to Sunday's fire. I mean, I didn't fall into it or anything, and it didn't do anything special except burn and save gas when Sarah didn't use her stove in the kitchen... But you see it is Sunday's fire that I remembered the most on our visits to the National Bahá'í Center. We would sit out by the fire as the evening grew dark. The fire would burn as Dad and Mom and Sarah and Sunday would talk quietly. I would stare into the fire and listen. It was while staring into this fire that I learned how Sarah became Bahá'í.

They had been studying the Faith in Guinea and Sunday had become a Bahá'í, but Sarah just couldn't accept that anyone could take the place of Jesus in her heart. Jesus made her happier than anything. She even had a picture of Him on her wall and she was sure Jesus looked exactly like that picture. Sitting in her small dark room Sarah was confused. She loved the Bahá'í Faith, she thought it was good, but Bahá'u'lláh... She just couldn't imagine Him. How could she love Him? The saintly face of Jesus was before her on the wall but she couldn't call up the face of Bahá'u'lláh. So she prayed.

That night she became very ill. In just a short time she knew her fever was dangerously high and she couldn't go out for help because she had a terrible pain in her stomach. She lay on her bed wondering whether the time had really come for her to die.

Her pain became worse; she couldn't bear it. She didn't know where to turn. Suddenly she sat upright and from her very soul she cried, "Bahá'u'lláh!" Her whole body heaved and she vomited on the floor beside her bed. She fell backwards, her eyes turned toward the ceiling, but instead of darkness she saw a brilliant blue heaven open up and before her, in the deepest silence she could imagine, a Man appeared with jet black hair. He smiled. His smile was so sweet that she felt her soul rush toward Him. Just as suddenly He disappeared, the heavens closed up and Sarah was in darkness. But the darkness was changed. Sarah was a Bahá'í. She had seen the face of Bahá'u'lláh.

Well, frankly this story seemed a little strange to me. I mean, thinking back to all the times I had thrown up I couldn't remember a time I had seen Bahá'u'lláh. But I would keep it in mind the next time I was sick.

Sarah still had her picture of Jesus on the wall in her bedroom. She even had a little table with two candles on it. I was confused by this because we had never had a picture of Jesus and a table with two candles on it, no matter how much we love Jesus. Mom says that it's not important because Sarah is a devoted Bahá'í (I mean, did *we* ever see Bahá'u'lláh?) and if she loves Jesus too, well, that's just wonderful.

Both Sarah and Sunday say that they never could remove the stain on the floor left by that experience, even after scrubbing for several days. I found that awfully interesting and am secretly dying to see it. I keep asking Mom and Dad if it wouldn't be nice to take a teaching trip to Guinea . . . but they say that our country is new to the Faith and we have plenty to do here. Mom looks at me suspiciously.

"Why are you so interested in Guinea?" she asks.

"Oh, no special reason," I answer, looking evasively into Sunday's fire.

The story of how Sarah became a Bahá'í is true.

PIECE OF CAKE

Josh sat at the cafeteria table nibbling his sandwich. Two of his fellow seventh graders were sitting nearby and he was trying to think of a good way to invite them to next Saturday's Bahá'í picnic. Josh always had trouble thinking of ways to teach the Faith and it didn't help that he was a bit on the shy side. Inviting his friends to a picnic seemed like a pretty good opening — after all, sooner or later they were bound to ask, "What's Bahá'í?" The trouble was, he was almost as shy about inviting them to a picnic as teaching the Faith itself.

Josh laid down his sandwich, took a gulp of milk and kind of inched his chair closer to them. "Hi!" he boomed cheerfully. Sally and Paula looked at him like he'd just descended from outer space. Josh mentally kicked himself, he'd just greeted them five minutes ago and now they'd think he was a real goon.

"Hi, again," said Sally dryly. She waited expectantly.

Might as well be direct, thought Josh. "Uh, I thought, I mean I was wondering . . ." Great, real direct.

"Yes?"

"I was just wondering if you two would be interested in coming to a . . . a Bahá'í picnic."

"Bahá'í picnic? What's Bahá'í?"

There, just like he thought – his opening. Piece of cake!

"It's a religion."

Sally's eyes narrowed. "What kind of religion?"

"Well, it's a religion that teaches that all religions come from the same God and . . ."

She interrupted, her eyes narrowing further, "Do you accept Christ as your personal Savior?"

"Well, uh . . . in a way." Wonderful, his piece of cake was turning out to be hard rock. Way to go, Josh, you know how to choose 'um.

"What do you mean, 'in a way'?" Sally's voice had an edge that told Josh that maybe he'd better go back to his sandwich. He looked back at it fleetingly, but then decided he'd better stick to it.

"What I mean is that yes, I do accept Christ as my personal Savior, but then there's also Moses, Muḥammad, Krishna, Buddha and all the other Prophets too. They're all my personal Saviors in a way."

"In a way . . ." Sally pushed her lunch tray away. Josh could see she had much more to say. He half expected her to roll up her sleeves.

Instead, she leaned over, looked him straight in the eye and said, "Don't you know that there is only one way? The way of our Lord Jesus Christ." She then calmly took a sip of milk. Josh guessed she was fortifying herself for further battle. He wondered what Paula thought and glanced her way.

"She feels the same way I do – she goes to the same church." Sally announced, having caught the glance.

Josh was in no way prepared to do battle. This wasn't because he couldn't hold his own, but simply because he knew that Bahá'ís should never argue about religion. He hesitated.

Piece of Cake

"Well?"

"Well, Sally, I think that's just wonderful that you love Jesus so much. In fact I do too." He thought maybe this would be a graceful exit and slowly began inching his way back to his sandwich, which was looking more appetizing by the minute. But Sally wouldn't let him off so easily.

"So, what about these other 'prophets'? Are you trying to tell me they're as good as Jesus?"

Josh knew now he couldn't let it go without some explanation. "It's just that we feel that God sent these other Prophets too – that the coming of all the Prophets, one after another, all over the world, is part of God's great plan."

"Josh," she said, neatly folding up her napkin and laying it on the tray, "these other 'prophets' you talk about *all* come straight from the devil – and everyone who follows them is *going* straight to the devil too."

At that Josh felt his first twinge of impatience. "Really Sally, you can't believe that. Now just look at Rahj there." He pointed down the table at his Hindu friend. "He's as kind, considerate and well-mannered as anyone... including you, and he's Hindu. You can't tell me he's going to the devil." Then he murmured, "even if there *were* a devil."

Sally, Josh was beginning to notice, didn't miss much. "*If* there were a devil!" She gazed at Josh sadly. "I'm afraid you'll find out soon enough whether there's a devil or not!"

At this Josh could hardly suppress a grin – but tried hard to look serious.

"Anyway Josh," she continued, "you know I can't hang around you any more, now that I know how you feel, or Rahj either. It would be against my faith."

Josh nodded solemnly. In a funny way he *was* sad,

A for Effort

as comic as she now sounded and as strange as Sally's views seemed to be. She'd always been fun to kid around with and that's why he had invited her.

Before he could answer, Eric and his "crowd" walked up. Eric was a wise guy and always seemed to need a group of kids around him. Josh wondered why he was so popular. He saw his friend Rahj at the edge of the crowd and waved to him.

"Hey Josh, you heard about my party Friday?" Eric asked loudly.

"Sure, I'll be there. I've already asked my parents."

"What about you, Sally, Paula?"

Sally didn't answer at first and Paula, as usual, seemed to look to her friend.

Finally Sally answered, "I don't go to parties."

Eric looked surprised. "Not to *any* parties?"

"You'll be dancing, won't you?"

"Why sure, that's what parties are for."

"I don't dance."

"That's no problem, Sally. I'll teach you to dance."

"I don't dance because I don't believe in dancing. Dancing is sinful," she said smugly.

Oh no, said Josh to himself, she said *that* to the wrong person. He gave Rahj, who was now standing beside him, an exasperated look.

Eric cocked his head. "Get this guys, dancing is *sinful!*"

"Well it is!" retorted Sally, "and you'll all be sorry some day you didn't listen to me!"

"So," Eric cooed, "Saintly Sally speaks – and we'll all be sorry!" He laughed out loud and predictably his friends laughed with him. Josh and Rahj remained silent.

Josh was feeling uncomfortable. He didn't see anything wrong with dancing but he felt sorry for Sally who had turned scarlet. He knew that she was in for a good ribbing from Eric for some time to come. And, if Eric ribbed her, a lot of his friends would join in.

"Well, Saintly Sally," Eric continued, "I'll tell you what. You stay home and pray for us and we'll take our chances at the party." He laughed and moved off, leaving Sally smoldering.

"You'll all go to the devil!" she exclaimed as a parting shot.

Eric merely laughed as he moved out into the corridor. They could hear echoes of "Saintly Sally!" all the way down the hall as he returned to class.

Josh and Rahj didn't quite know what to say after that. As it was, they didn't have to say anything. Sally gave them one indignant look and, Paula in tow, flounced off to class.

Josh was right. The matter didn't stop there. Soon the whole class knew about Sally's beliefs and many amused glances were cast her way. Not only that, but Eric never missed a chance to taunt her. In the days that followed Sally seemed to withdraw with Paula as her only friend. They sat alone in the cafeteria and stuck together at all times – seeming to shun anyone else's company. Josh thought this was a bad tactic. If she just acted normally, everyone would eventually forget the whole thing.

He talked it over with Rahj one day and they decided they would try to draw her out. They found Sally and Paula in the cafeteria and sat down beside them. Four days had passed since Josh had tried to invite them to the picnic and aside from an occasional hello, this was the first time he had tried to talk to them.

"Hi, what's up?" said Josh cheerfully.

A for Effort

"Hi!" answered Paula enthusiastically. Sally eyed her with disapproval but answered in turn. Josh guessed that maybe Paula was getting tired of spending all her time alone with Sally and welcomed some company.

Rahj tried to break the ice, "Are you coming to the basketball game on Saturday night?"

Josh couldn't imagine Sally would have any objection to that and was relieved when Paula answered, "Yeah, Sally and I are going with her parents."

"Think we'll win?" asked Josh lamely, not knowing what else to say.

"Maybe," answered Sally grudgingly.

Josh took a deep breath, wondering how to begin. "Say, why are you girls always alone these days?"

"It seems like no one wants to talk to *us*, and we don't care. We have our church friends," Sally answered coolly.

"Aw Sally, everybody likes you. It's just Eric and his crowd that are giving you a hard time. It'll pass. If you stop talking to *everyone*, people will think you're strange and stuck-up."

"Everyone who truly follows Christ's path seems strange to others. We don't mind."

"Oh, come on. Following Christ's path means loving everyone. You can't love everyone if you don't talk to them."

Josh caught a glitter of agreement in Paula's eyes and this encouraged him. "Anyway, everyone misses the way you used to kid around."

Sally looked up at that. She seemed to melt just a little bit. "What makes you think that?"

"Well, we all feel that way."

Suddenly the bell rang and seemed to be a good excuse for Sally not to answer. She got up and collected her tray. "Gotta go," she said, "see you in class."

Paula got up more slowly and when Sally's back was turned she glanced up at Josh with a brief smile. "Thanks," she said.

Josh and Rahj seemed to have broken the ice a bit. For the rest of the day both Sally and Paula were more friendly to those around them and at least didn't seem so glum.

But Josh hadn't counted on Eric putting a cloud over it all. When history was over at the end of the day and the final bell rang, Eric got up and sauntered over to Sally.

"Hey, Saintly Sally! Said any prayers for me lately. Maybe you can *save* my *soul*!" At those last three words he placed his hands over his heart and gazed heavenwards, rolling his eyes. Some of the other kids laughed. Sally turned red and tried to ignore him.

Up until then, Josh had never interfered, but suddenly he felt Eric had gone too far. He stepped in.

"Eric."

Eric, still grinning from ear to ear, turned toward Josh. "Yeah?"

"Why don't you just make fun of me. I mean, I'm a Bahá'í and I'm different too — or Rahj here, he doesn't eat pork. You can laugh at us too."

One by one the laughing crowd quieted down. Everyone looked at the two boys facing each other. Eric's grin faded.

"But . . ." he hesitated, then with more courage he said, "But you don't act like you're better than everyone else. And Rahj keeps to himself."

"But that's not the point," said Josh, softening his tone a bit. "You're not making fun of her just because she thinks she's better than everyone else. You're

A for Effort

making fun of her religion. That's different, Eric. That's what's wrong."

For the first time since he had known him, Josh saw what looked like shame on Eric's face. He lowered his head. "I didn't mean anything . . ."

Josh sighed and sat down at the desk. He couldn't win. He wanted to help Sally but now he'd just made Eric feel bad. "I know, Eric, you were just having fun. Maybe you don't know how it feels to have people make fun of your religion, but," he said glancing at Sally who quickly lowered her eyes, "I do. When people make cracks about me being a Bahá'í, well, it hurts a little. I know how it feels and I just don't like seeing other people being hurt too. Everyone has a right to their own beliefs."

Eric looked up at Josh. "All right, I know what you mean. But maybe you can tell *her* that just because she's different doesn't mean that she's better." At that he picked up his books and walked toward the door. Then, just as he passed through, he turned and shot Josh one of his famous 'Eric' grins. "See you around, Josh, like at my party tonight."

"Sure thing," Josh called back with a relieved smile.

The silence which had taken hold of the classroom was broken as everyone bustled around, collecting their things and filing out. Everyone but Sally, Paula and Josh.

Sally rose to leave. She picked up her books, sighed and then said abruptly, "You're not a bad guy, Josh, even if you are a Bahá'í."

Josh thought she was making a joke, but as he searched her face for some trace of a smile, there was none. Sally was perfectly serious. Before he could answer she left.

Piece of Cake

Josh tried not to look at Paula as he piled his books on top of one another, and Paula didn't seem too anxious to talk, but she didn't seem to want to leave either. Finally, as Josh headed toward the door, she asked in a small voice, "What time did you say that picnic was?"

Josh stopped short, not sure he had heard right. But he knew he had when he saw Paula's timid smile.

"11:30 Saturday morning. Rock Creek Park, on the left as you come in." He paused. "My parents can give you a lift if you need one."

"I'll have to see if my parents agree..."

"Sure," said Josh, "I'll give you a call." And he left, hiding just a trace of a smile as he ducked through the door.

Piece of cake, he thought to himself, and whistled all the way to the school bus.

SOME SUMMER...

"They're here, Dad," yelled Sandy as she raced to the door. It opened with a bang and Sandy skidded to a stop on the creaky cabin porch, catching herself just in time to avoid tumbling down the steps.

She looked expectantly at her uncle's old Buick, which rolled to a stop in the driveway, and caught her breath, as her cousin, Raphaël emerged from the car.

Well, la di *da!* she murmured to herself. Cousin Raphaël was not what she expected. Dressed in an elegant cotton pants suit, of a subtle shade of turquoise and with dainty heels, Raphaël gracefully glided across the yard. Sandy took in the exquisite pink scarf and sighed. This is going to be *some* summer, she thought glumly.

Then she noticed her cousin Jean Marie who hopped out of the other side of the car. He, in contrast, was more reassuring in well-worn jeans and a tee shirt.

Sandy stepped forward as they came up the steps, acutely conscious of her tattered jeans and the stained apron which she had forgotten to take off.

"Hi!" She held out her hand, "I'm Sandy."

"I'm very pleased to meet you," answered Raphaël carefully as she glanced at Sandy's clothes.

"I'm Jean Marie," said her other cousin. He shook her hand vigorously.

Sandy's father opened the door and smiled warmly at his niece and nephew. He was tall and tanned and his smile always set off attractive wrinkles in the corners of his eyes. Sandy was proud of him and noticed how dignified he looked even in casual clothes.

"Well, you finally made it! Must have been a long trip."

"Yes," answered Raphaël.

"Oh!" exclaimed Jean Marie as Uncle Sam struggled up the steps with the two big, heavy suitcases. "*Pardon!*" He reached down to take one of them.

"That's okay. A little exercise never hurt anyone." With one last effort he hauled the two suitcases on to the porch. He wiped his forehead with one of his crisp white hankerchiefs that never failed to amaze Sandy. Uncle Sam was a widower, did his own washing and ironing and despite his numerous activities, always turned out spotless. "Hi, Tom. How's the book coming?"

"I've hit a few snags but it's coming along." Sandy's father was a writer of instruction manuals for computers. Sandy, who was an aspiring writer herself, couldn't think of anything more boring. But, she conceded, someone had to do it. And if anyone could make sense of those infernal machines, he could.

"Hey Snoopy," said Uncle Sam, addressing Sandy, "What's for lunch?" Sandy smiled at the nickname. Her uncle had been calling her that since she was two. It was derived, not from the famous comic strip character but from her incessant curiosity.

Suddenly her face froze in horror. "Lunch! Not again!" she wailed as she burst through the door, ran through the living-room and into the smoke-filled kitchen. A minute later she reappeared.

"What *was* for lunch, dear?" asked Uncle Sam, a mischievous smile playing on his lips.

"Hamburgers," muttered Sandy.

Raphaël grimaced and shot Jean Marie a glance which said clearly, "What did I tell you?" She immediately replaced the grimace with a smile but not quickly enough. Sandy noticed it.

"What's the matter? You don't like hamburgers?"

"Oh, *non, non*," she said hastily, "Uh . . ."

Jean Marie interrupted, "We know you Americans eat hamburgers – we've tried some in Paris . . ."

"And?"

"Uh, they were very . . . interesting." Now if Sandy had known that "interesting" in French was more of a compliment it might have made her feel better.

"Oh," she said.

"Well, look," said her father, "it seems perhaps your first meal here has run into some unexpected difficulties. Why don't we run down to the new Kentucky Fried Chicken that's just opened in town?"

Sandy threw him a grateful glance. Dad was wonderful and always knew when to come to the rescue.

"And this evening you're all invited to my humble home for dinner," announced Uncle Sam.

Well that takes care of day one, said Sandy to herself. She hated to cook but had acquired the detested chore since they arrived. Mother had stayed behind to be with her brother who was attending summer school. Dad helped sometimes but it made her feel guilty. He was working so hard on his book.

Sandy awoke from her thoughts to find Raphaël looking at her strangely as everyone else was heading for the car. She looked down at her clothes and sighed, "Guess I'd better change. I won't be a minute."

She dressed hurriedly but was careful to choose something a little more stylish. In a few minutes they were all in Uncle Sam's car heading down the road. Sandy kept her thoughts to herself as she stared out the window. She was deeply disappointed about how the summer was working out. Sandy was a Bahá'í and had made exciting plans to attend Green Acre Bahá'í Summer School, followed by a Canadian travel teaching trip to Quebec with a youth group. She had been working hard on her French and was looking forward to what would have been an inspiring and interesting experience.

Then suddenly they received news from her uncle in France that he would like to send his children for their first visit to the States. Sandy was flabbergasted when she learned she was expected to cancel her plans and entertain cousins she had never met before. Her parents were not Bahá'ís but they were very tolerant and were impressed by the changes in her since she met the Bahá'ís in her town. After discussing the matter over with the Local Spiritual Assembly, they had agreed that she could go to Green Acre and Quebec. Now it was all off. Just like that. No one ever thought about *her*.

Uncle Sam interrupted her thoughts, "Hey kids, do you know any American songs? How about, 'I've Been Working on the Railroad'?"

"Good grief!" thought Sandy as she crouched deeper into her seat.

Uncle Sam was a doll – but sometimes . . . Actually he was the one who introduced her to the Faith. Of an already decidedly unorthodox family, he was the most unorthodox. Everyone thought he was a bit

Some Summer . . .

strange, but everyone loved him, Sandy most of all. She had been his pet since she was a toddler. One day last summer, when she was a bit down, he had asked her if she ever thought about God. The question surprised her. What had God got to do with it? Uncle Sam didn't answer right away. He sat on the porch whittling away on his statue. Wood carving was how he made his living out here in the boondocks, and he did quite well for himself. Then he had asked, "Well, have you ever thought about your soul?"

Her soul? Now this was even more off beat. But Uncle Sam went on to explain that we must have been put on this earth for some reason and since our soul was the most permanent part of our make-up, maybe we should spend more time paying attention to it. What he said began to make sense. Sandy had always believed in God but had long since stopped going to church. But when he got to the part about all religions coming from one God, something had clicked. Why, this sounded almost reasonable.

Then Sandy had asked, "Does this have anything to do with your Bahá'í religion?"

"Well, as a matter of fact, it does," Uncle Sam had said with a smile.

In the long summer days that followed, Sandy learned all about the Báb, Bahá'u'lláh and 'Abdu'l-Bahá, and when she got back home she looked up the local Bahá'ís.

Her parents had smiled tolerantly when she started going to meetings, but were pleasantly surprised when they met the Bahá'ís and saw what a good influence they had on her character. Why, she had become *almost* civil to her little brother!

Speaking of character, she realized that she was

being a bit of a wet blanket. She broke from her reverie and joined in the song.

"Fee fi fiddle-i-ie-oh! Fee fi fiddle-i-ie-oh oh oh!"

Good grief! she thought to herself again and smiled pleasantly at Raphaël who was having a bit of trouble with her "fis".

When they got to the restaurant and were seated, Raphaël looked around. "Fast food?" she asked.

"Yeah, I guess so," said Sandy.

"Americans always eat fast food. In France we spend many hours to cook. To cook is an art. To eat is an art."

"Oh," said Sandy, "well, I would think you waste a lot of time cooking." She wrinkled up her nose.

Jean Marie rejoined, "If you cook quickly, who would want to waste time to eat this food?"

Raphaël's attention was diverted by a family which had just come in the door. The woman had curlers in her hair, an old tee shirt, short shorts and flip flops.

"They say you Americans go out like this – but I didn't believe it. Look at the . . . things in her hair."

"Curlers," said Sandy.

"Curlers! Before everybody!"

"You don't have to look at her, you know."

"Do *you* go out with . . . curlers in your hair?"

"Me personally? No, but she's free to do what she likes. This is a free country, you know."

"In France, we dress well to go out."

Sandy looked pointedly at Jean Marie. "Everybody?"

Raphaël understood and said, "That shirt was very expensive. I myself bought it – and the jeans are Jordache!"

"American, I see," replied Sandy smugly.

Raphaël, clearly bested, shook her silky blond head and sank into a sullen silence.

Uncle Sam, who had been watching this exchange with some anxiety, beamed benevolently. "Well, dears, fast food or no, we're hungry and I really think you'll like it." He took their orders and went up to the cashier.

When they got back to the house, Uncle Sam dropped them off. "Don't forget, dinner at my place at 5:30."

"5:30?" asked Raphaël, bewildered.

"Yeah," said Sandy.

"You eat at 5:30?"

"Sure, when do you eat?"

"Usually we eat about 8:00."

"Well," answered Sandy, as she pulled the screen door open, "I'm afraid we can't rearrange Uncle Sam's plans."

She went into the kitchen and surveyed the mess with dismay. She started to clean up, dropping the scorched hamburgers in the trash. Seconds later she found Raphaël by her side, putting dishes into the sink.

"Oh, that's okay. I'll do it," Sandy said, embarrassed to have Raphaël see her failure first hand.

"I like to work in the kitchen," she answered as she filled the sink with water. Sandy said nothing and soon everything was washed up.

Sandy went to get sheets to make up Raphaël and Jean Marie's beds. Raphaël would be sleeping in her room and Jean Marie would be sleeping in her father's room. Again Sandy found Raphaël next to her, helping with the beds. She said nothing. When they had finished, Sandy did some general straight-

A for Effort

ening up. Raphaël went into the living-room and was soon playing cards with Jean Marie.

Well, thought Sandy, as she finished shaking out a rug on the back porch, I guess I should show them a good time. She went into the living room.

"I thought you all might like to go down and see the river."

Without looking up from her cards, Raphaël said, "We're playing cards."

"Oh," said Sandy, "Maybe you'd like to change into something more comfortable?"

"Why?" said Raphaël, "I'm very comfortable. Do I not look comfortable?"

Sandy couldn't imagine anyone being comfortable in those heels but said nothing.

That suits me just fine, she thought to herself as she went back into her room to dig out her notebooks. She settled in the backyard in a tree and started working on a new story.

Dinner time came quickly and Dad emerged from his study. "About time to go?" he yelled out the back door.

"Sure," said Sandy as she dropped down out of the tree.

Raphaël and Jean Marie were still playing cards when Sandy walked into the living-room. "Time to go," she said.

With a resigned look Raphaël gathered up the cards and stood up. Jean Marie ran his fingers through his hair and smiled.

"Hamburgers tonight?"

"I would think not," said Sandy's father. "Uncle Sam is a good cook. He may surprise you."

"Oh! A gourmet!"

"Yes, a gourmet," said Sandy.

Some Summer . . .

Uncle Sam's cabin was one of Sandy's favorite places. Nestled in a grove of pine trees, you hardly noticed it until you were right upon it.

"Well, you *did* come!" called Uncle Sam from the porch. He laid down an exquisite statue of dark African wood that he'd been working on.

"Wouldn't miss it!" yelled Sandy. As she approached the steps she said, "But I did expect to find you cooking."

"A good cook prepares well in advance and usually only has to attend to last minute details right before dinner."

"You can get to those last minute details right now; we're hungry," said Sandy's father as he tromped up the steps.

"I thought I'd show our guests around a little first. They're probably not used to eating this early."

Raphaël glanced at Jean Marie and beamed, "A civilized man!"

"Well, I guess that depends on what civilization you're talking about. Now in Indonesia . . ."

"Oh, Uncle Sam, don't show off. We know you know everything!" Sandy said in mock exasperation.

"Everything? Now that's quite a compliment."

"I suppose by showing us around you mean you're going to take us into your snake's den." Sandy grinned and sneaked a look at Raphaël out of the corner of her eye, certain that Raphaël's type wouldn't be interested in snakes.

To her surprise Raphaël smiled in delight. "Oh," she said, "Do you collect snakes?"

"Sure, you like snakes?"

"I love all animals. I'm going to be a veterinarian."

'Well then, Raphaël, we'll get along just fine. Come along."

A for Effort

Sandy trailed along in dismay. It was surprising for a tomboy like her, but she just couldn't get over her fear of snakes. She'd really tried, to please Uncle Sam, but every time she saw them slithering in their cages, or even worse, out of their cages, she recoiled in horror.

She was happy to note that Jean Marie didn't look overly enthusiastic either, and she chatted with him on the way to the shed, more to cover up her nervousness than for anything else. But Jean Marie didn't seem to be in a chatting mood. She'd noticed that despite his humor and natural enthusiasm, he often fell into this silent state and it irritated her.

Uncle Sam and Raphaël went into the shed while Sandy and Jean Marie stood at the door. Sandy pretended to be absorbed in conversation with Jean Marie, which wasn't easy as he only answered in monosyllables.

Uncle Sam took Raphaël from cage to cage, making comments about this snake and that. Raphaël, surprising Sandy, knew quite a lot about them. Then they opened up a cage. Sandy stopped her discourse in mid-sentence and watched nervously. They had opened the cage of the Boa. Raphaël reached in and carefully, expertly, eased it out on to her shoulder. Sandy shuddered. Raphaël's face lit up with joy.

Soon they replaced the Boa and still in deep conversation made their way out of the shed. Sandy and Jean Marie walked behind them silently. She'd given up all attempts to engage him in conversation. Then, to her total amazement, Jean Marie stopped and asked, "Sandy, what is Bahá'í?"

"Uh ... Bahá'í?"

"Yes, my father told us Uncle Sam is Bahá'í." He blushed. "He said it's some strange religion."

Some Summer . . .

"Oh," said Sandy. She hesitated, "It's not *that* strange. It's a universal religion. In other words we accept the truth of all major religions."

"Is it a sect?"

"No, it's an independent religion. We work toward universal peace. We try to promote understanding and unity between different races, nations and religions of the world."

"We? You're Bahá'í too?"

"Yes, I am," she said feeling distinctly uncomfortable. She hadn't been much of an example up to this point.

"Oh," said Jean Marie, blushing again. "I hope I did not offend you."

"No, not at all." Sandy smiled. "Lot's of people think it's strange at first."

"But," he continued, "how can you unite all religions? They're so different."

Sandy launched into an explanation of progressive revelation and was just warming up when she found Raphaël beside her.

"You talk of religion?" she smirked.

"Yes," said Sandy defensively, "I was just explaining the Bahá'í Faith."

"You are . . . Bahá'í, too?"

Sandy didn't answer but continued her explanation where she had left off.

But soon her father, who had declined a look at snakes he had already seen often enough, called out the door of the house. "Are you going to talk all day or are you planning to eat?"

"Ah food!" said Jean Marie and headed toward the door. Resigned, Sandy followed.

Uncle Sam had outdone himself with an elegant four-course French dinner, complete with candles and music by a popular French singer playing softly in the background.

With each new course their French guests lit up with pleasure.

"This is not possible, where did you learn French cuisine?" exclaimed Raphaël.

"It's one of his many hobbies," said Sandy dryly. She couldn't understand why Uncle Sam went to so much trouble to prepare French food. Why, they should be exposed to American food and habits. They were already so snobbish about their "cuisine", she didn't think they should be encouraged. But she made the best of it and did try to be pleasant. After all, she thought, they know I'm a Bahá'í. I guess I should try and act like one.

She even complimented the French dishes, though the words almost stuck in her throat. "Do you eat like this every day?"

"No, not every day," said Raphaël with regret. "We have no time to always prepare like this. We do when we can, especially for guests."

When dinner was over, Uncle Sam, her father and Raphaël talked about Raphaël's plans to become a veterinarian. Jean Marie, having seemingly expended all his enthusiasm on dinner, sat quietly reading. Sandy, seated in front of the fireplace, stared at the fire glumly. A whole summer wasted, she thought.

When the time came to leave, Sandy said, "I think I'll stay and chat with Uncle Sam for a while. I can walk home. It isn't far."

"Well, okay," said Dad and he and her cousins left. When they were alone Sandy didn't speak immediately but continued to stare at the fire. Uncle Sam seemed content to leave her to her own thoughts.

Finally she said, "They're so snobbish about their French food, why do you encourage them?"

Uncle Sam seemed surprised. "Why, I wanted them to feel at home. To make them happy." Then he said gently, "Is something wrong with that?"

"Oh no!" said Sandy slapping her knees in frustration. "It's just that here I am wasting my whole summer with people who don't even appreciate this beautiful country. I had such wonderful plans, Uncle Sam!" She looked at him with pleading eyes. "Can't you see what I had to give up just to hold their hands when they don't even like me?"

"Have you tried to appreciate *their* culture? You could at least practice your French."

"They'd just make fun of me."

"On the contrary, they'd probably appreciate your efforts."

Sandy sighed, "Maybe."

"I'm sure you've heard this before, Sandy, but things don't always turn out how we would like."

"But my plans were for the Faith! Doesn't God appreciate that?"

"Maybe He wants you to serve in another way. And maybe He wants you to learn a few things in the process."

Uncle Sam put his stockinged feet on the coffee table. "Believe me, sweetheart, one thing you'll learn is that we can't always serve exactly how we want to. I know a wonderful Bahá'í teacher who would love to spend all his time teaching, but he has been called to serve on a sacred institution. And because he's so trustworthy, he's also serving on one committee after another. He doesn't stop teaching, but in these days, when our numbers are so limited, we are called upon

A for Effort

to do all sorts of things we think we're not suited to do. I know that's not your case..."

"Uncle Sam," interrupted Sandy, her chin in her hands, "that's something I've wanted to ask you. You're such a good Bahá'í, why don't *you* go on teaching trips?"

Uncle Sam seemed a bit taken aback by this question but he smiled. "A very good question, Sandy. All of us are called upon to teach. It's our most sacred duty. But that doesn't mean we all teach in the same way. You know I'm a homefront pioneer, don't you?"

"Why no, I never thought about it."

"I chose this small town some years ago when there were no Bahá'ís in the area. I chose it because I felt that my own way of teaching was suited for this area."

"You mean there were *no* Bahá'ís here when you came? Why, you've got a big community here now. Did *you* make them Bahá'ís?"

Uncle Sam seemed a bit uncomfortable. "Well, honey, none of us 'make' Bahá'ís, that's all in God's hands. But slowly our community grew."

"But you don't seem to go out of your way to teach. I hardly ever notice you mentioning the Faith."

"Oh, I do, Sandy, I do. But now most people know I'm a Bahá'í. It's a small town. So I do my best to live the Bahá'í life – we don't always have to speak with words."

"Everybody loves you."

"If it were a larger town I would teach more. As a matter of fact, I'm thinking of leaving. There's a strong LSA here now..."

"So you'll go to another small town?"

"Yes, maybe."

"Where?"

"South America."

Sandy's eyes grew wide. "But Uncle Sam, it's so far, I'd never *see* you."

"Well, I would come back from time to time. Anyway, nothing's sure. I still have to find a way to make a living there."

"Uncle Sam," said Sandy suddenly, "you should get married again."

Again Uncle Sam was taken aback. But he recovered quickly. "Well, now that it's all out in the open, Snoopy, maybe I should say that may be part of the 'arrangements' I'm making."

"No!" exclaimed Sandy.

"I didn't think I could ever marry again after your Aunt Mary died, but . . ."

"You've found someone? Is she a Bahá'í?"

"You know her."

Sandy's face was infused with delight. "Christine! Why she'd make a lovely pioneer!"

"You *are* perceptive, aren't you, dear?"

"And she speaks Spanish."

"Her family's in Peru."

"You're certainly full of surprises tonight!" said Sandy, her chin sinking back into her hands as she stared into the fire.

"I'm always full of surprises, Sandy. But I think we've strayed from the subject. We were talking about you and the present situation you find yourself in."

"Oh, that."

"Yes, that. I think you can turn it into a spiritual exercise."

"I'm sure you do," said Sandy dismally.

"Listen, I've got a theory. Actually it's not my own completely – it comes straight from the Bahá'í writings. You know that everyone is made in the image of God, right?"

"Well..."

"Bahá'u'lláh says so..."

"Well, if Bahá'u'lláh says so, I guess I can't argue, can I?" said Sandy smiling.

"Now, from my own experience I can see that. The older I get the more I see that each human being is unique. Every human being is beautiful in their own way. Every human being reflects, even in some small way, the image of God."

"Hmmm..." grunted Sandy.

"Now look, Sandy," Uncle Sam continued. "Did you see the pleasure reflected in Raphaël's face when she held that snake? That smile was like a ray of light. It lit up the room. Did you notice it?"

"Yes, I guess I did."

"But you dismissed it. You didn't appreciate it, you didn't savor it. Why? because you were so busy thinking of her negative aspects."

"Well, you're right," said Sandy, shamefaced.

"Don't be ashamed," said Uncle Sam with a gentle smile. "It's a normal reaction these days. From the time we're born it's almost like we're trained to have these reactions. Now dear, you know that we have a new Revelation from God. And the purpose of this Revelation is to change the hearts of men, to create a new race of men. And in the Bahá'í teachings we have everything we need to do this. We must start with our own hearts. 'Abdu'l-Bahá says that if someone has ten negative qualities and one good quality, we must forget the ten and look at the one good."

"I know, we read that in our last deepening."

"Now, what that does is start a chain reaction."

"A chain reaction?"

"Yes, now think. Let's say you don't like someone very much. Quite naturally this person probably doesn't like you very much because they sense these negative feelings.

"Now, what would happen if you made a special effort to find one good quality in that person? *And* at the same time you complimented that person on it?"

"They would probably be suspicious!"

"Perhaps in the beginning. But if you were sincere and tried to show it, they would probably believe you."

"Maybe."

"Now, if they believed you, they would probably be surprised at first. Then they would feel some small pleasure and they would probably smile and thank you."

"Yes,..."

"This smile is the key. It's very hard to dislike someone when they're smiling at you."

"I guess so."

"So, you see, when they smile at you and thank you, they will be more likeable. And, at least for that small instant, you will like them better.

"And, if you like them and they sense it, they will probably find it in their heart to like you – for that moment, at least.

"Okay."

"So, dear, you have established a moment of mutual respect. You will have made that person feel **good** about themselves – more likeable. You will have **produced** a positive reaction.

"Now, let's say you continued in this manner. People are very sensitive, believe it or not. If you consistently dismiss all negative thoughts about this person, they are going to sense it. You see, the reason this person probably didn't like you in the first place is because you made them feel defensive about their bad qualities."

"Okay Uncle Sam, you're making sense – sounds like you've been taking some psychology courses."

"It all comes from reading the writings and trying to apply them."

"So, what you mean is that if I sincerely try to like a person, they are going to like me. And if they like me better, well, I'm going to like them even better because this will make them more likeable. A chain reaction, as you say."

"Absolutely. But in the end the word is love. 'Abdu'l-Bahá's love for each person was unconditional and each and every person, in the end, succumbed to it's influence."

Sandy ran a hand through her short blond hair and then stood up. "I'm going to try, Uncle Sam, I'm really going to try." She turned towards the door.

"But," Uncle Sam called out as she reached the door, "it's not easy. It takes practice. I like to say it takes spiritual exercise. We need to exercise those spiritual muscles."

Sandy grinned. "You always were original, Uncle Sam."

"Unique!" he called out, laughing.

The next day at breakfast, Sandy tried to be cheerful, even though Raphaël had looked disdainfully at the breakfast cereal and only drank coffee.

Her father noticed it. "You're all bright-eyed and bushy-tailed this morning. What's on the agenda for you young folks?"

"Well, I thought I'd take Raphaël and Jean Marie

out on the river in the boat. We could get in a little fishing."

Jean Marie, crunching a mouthful of cereal nodded vigorously. Raphaël didn't look too excited.

Jean Marie explained. "Raphaël doesn't like boats *or* fish."

"She doesn't have to fish and we're certain to see all sorts of interesting wildlife in these parts. It's really very beautiful out on the river."

Raphaël looked mollified. But Sandy's father warned, "You know you can't go far. It's very easy to get lost. The river branches out in many places and if you take a wrong turning it might take us days to find you."

"Don't worry, Dad, I know the area."

"You may *think* you know the area."

"Well, we'll be careful."

As Sandy and Raphaël were in the bedroom getting ready, Sandy turned to her and blurted out, "You know, Raphaël, you really know how to dress well. I mean, I wish I knew how to choose clothes as well as you do. I usually just take the first thing off the rack."

Raphaël turned toward Sandy slowly, looked at her directly in the eyes and studied her for a moment. Sandy knew she was wondering if she were sincere and she also knew she was. All morning she had been preparing herself for this one comment, trying very hard to overcome her pride.

Then Raphaël said slowly, "In France we try to dress nicely. It's a sign of respect to visitors and those who you visit."

"I guess it's not a bad custom." Sandy blushed, "Maybe I could use a few lessons."

And then it happened. A hesitant, timid smile

A for Effort

spread across Raphaël's face. "Perhaps we could have a time to go shopping together."

"That would be very nice," Sandy said warmly, "That would be very nice." She turned away quickly, pretending to look for something in her drawer. But her smile did not fade. One step had been taken and that one timid smile had touched her.

As they left the room together, Sandy was impressed by one thought – the key is humility.

They all made their way down to the boat, carrying fishing equipment and a large picnic basket for lunch. They had promised to be back shortly after they had eaten and even Raphaël now seemed enthusiastic. But when the moment came for her to step into the boat, Sandy noticed a look of sheer panic on her face.

Why, she's really afraid of the water! she thought in surprise. It was hard to resist a small tug of satisfaction. Raphaël had made her feel such a coward about snakes. But pity struck and she pushed these thoughts aside.

"Here, I'll help you. Jean Marie, you take one hand and I'll take the other." They helped her on to the small row boat and seated her near the back.

Soon they were off, Sandy taking the oars first, Jean Marie perched up near the front of the boat and Raphaël sitting uneasily in the back.

"I know a good pool where we can fish. I found it last summer. It's not far and I don't think many people go there." They rowed on in silence. It was a beautiful day, the sun shone brightly and the water, rippled by the cool wind, glistened in its reflection.

After a while they came to a place where the river branched off in two places. Sandy paused for a moment. "I think it's the one on the left."

"You don't know?" Raphaël asked tensely.

"Oh, I'm pretty sure."

"Why don't you ask those fishermen?" Raphaël pointed and Sandy turned to see another boat much like their own.

"They're so far off... Don't worry! We won't get lost. Anyway they probably don't know about this particular fishing hole and I wouldn't like to advertise it."

Sandy took up the oars again and took the left turning. They rowed on for some time. "So this must be the last turning on the right, or maybe it's the next," she mused. She rowed on a bit further. "Yes, I think I remember it. I came here with my brother last summer."

She turned into a much smaller branch. Trees were overhanging from each side and provided pleasant shade. They soon came to a deep pool.

"That's funny, it's not like I remember it. But it does look nice. Let's try here."

So Sandy and Jean Marie got out their poles and Sandy opened the tackle box for bait. In their manoeuvering, the boat rocked a little and Raphaël clutched at the sides.

"I think I will get out and sit over there on the..."

"On the bank. Okay, let me bring the boat closer so you can get out." She adeptly slid the boat close to the bank and Raphaël, with much trepidation, hopped out. She sat down on a log and looked infinitely more content. Sandy and Jean Marie cast their lines in the water and were soon getting some hopeful nibbles.

Suddenly Jean Marie got a firm bite and after a few minutes expertly pulled in a fine trout.

"Not bad," said Sandy enviously, "now it's my turn." But she wasn't having much luck and after

A for Effort

a good hour she announced in resignation, "Lunch time."

"Can we eat here on the bank?" asked Raphaël.

"Fine," said Sandy and she and Jean Marie hauled the heavy basket out of the boat.

Sandy passed out the clam and cheese sandwiches she had taken such pains to prepare early that morning. She was dismayed to see they had gone a bit soggy. "Not the best in the world," said said with as much humility as she could muster, "but it should fill us up."

Raphaël brought the limp sandwich to her mouth and after one bite replaced it in the waxed paper. "If Americans were, just one time, to try French bread, they would never eat this . . ."

"Mush," completed Jean Marie, quite apparently proud of his vocabulary. But he ate his with gusto nonetheless.

Sandy sat very still. She had really tried to make a nice lunch. How much effort was expected of her? She analyzed her feelings. She felt hurt. Why? Because she'd tried to please them and they didn't appreciate it . . . or was there another reason? Sandy knew there was. She was a horrible cook and she felt defensive about it. Why didn't she admit it to herself? It didn't mean she was a horrible person. So what if she was a horrible cook, she could admit it to the world and make light of it. One thing she was sure, if she kept trying to prove otherwise she'd always be miserable.

So there again was the key – humility. Pride kept her on the defensive. She felt a great weight lifted from her.

"I guess I can't hide it from the world any more," she laughed. "I'm a hopeless cook. Maybe I could use

Some Summer . . .

some lessons in that too, Raphaël," she said seriously. "Would you like to try?"

To Sandy's surprise Raphaël blushed and looked ashamed. "Sandy, I am sorry. I offended you. I do not want to say you are a bad cook."

"But I am!" she laughed. "I'm as bad as they come!"

"So," Raphaël hesitated, "if you like we could cook dinner together tonight."

"That would be great." Sandy looked around. "Well, we'd better get packed up."

When everything was in the boat, Jean Marie insisted on taking the oars and off they set in the direction in which they had come. On the way Sandy tried to practice her French. She knew she was butchering the language but they were very patient with her.

"I wish I could speak French as well as you speak English."

"Father is American, and even though he has become very French, he often speaks to us in English so we can practice. But we still do mistakes. Mostly the problem is vocabulary and American expressions. Father thought you could help us this summer."

At that point they reached the first branch of the river. Jean Marie rowed toward the left.

"No, Jean Marie, we need to go to the right."

"Sandy, I think you are mistaken. We came from the left."

Sandy paused a moment and then said, "No, I'm pretty sure we go right here. Let's try it for a while."

Jean Marie nodded doubtfully and shifted their course to the right.

"Now, after we pass one branch to the left we take the next one," she said.

"But I was sure our first turning was to the left, we should go now to the right."

Sandy had never been big on directions but she thought she recognized this part of the river and decided to trust her own instincts. Unfortunately they were wrong and very soon they were totally disoriented. Several hours passed as they tried one turning after another with no luck. Then, worse still, the stream they had turned into seemed to be petering out. There was a sudden lurch and the boat was mired in the mud.

"We'll have to get out and push."

But even in two feet of water Raphaël looked so panicked that Sandy insisted she stay in the boat while they pushed. After a good bit of pushing and shoving the boat was off again in the direction in which they had come. But it was now getting dark and they all began to feel jittery.

It was then that they passed under an overhanging branch. Sandy felt something much heavier and smoother than a twig slip from a tree on to her arm and into the boat. They all heard the thump when it landed. Sandy peered through the gathering darkness and saw something moving in the bottom of the boat.

"A snake!" she gasped. Involuntarily she jumped up, rocking the boat and terrifying Raphaël who screamed.

Then Sandy got a hold of herself and said as calmly as she could, "Raphaël, I don't know anything about snakes. Is there any way you could get it out?"

"I . . . I can't move. The boat will turn over – I can't!" she sobbed.

"Jean Marie . . ."

"I will try."

Some Summer . . .

But as he started to move toward the front of the boat it swayed madly.

"Oh, don't! Don't move!" cried Raphaël.

"Just stay there!" said Sandy.

Though Sandy had calmed herself to the point where she wasn't screaming, she was petrified and much too frightened to move, let alone try to get a snake out of the boat. Slowly and very softly she started saying 'The Remover of Difficulties'. She didn't even stop to think how strange it might sound to her cousins. Then slowly she mounted the seat plank in the front of the boat. The boat rocked and Raphaël let out another sob. She reached up and grabbed a branch and, as carefully as she could, tried to break it off. Luckily it was a dead branch and fairly brittle, but it still took some effort to break it, especially as she had to be careful not to rock the boat. With one final tug it came loose but sent her tumbling backwards into Jean Marie. Raphaël shrieked again.

Sandy righted herself and carefully stripped the stick of all loose twigs. She took a deep breath and looked down into the bottom of the boat. It was still light enough to see what appeared to Sandy as a slithering grotesque form. To her relief, she saw it was gliding up the side of the boat. With great care she brought the stick under it and with one quick motion flipped it over the side. It was gone!

Sandy let out one brief cry of relief and plopped down in a heap on the seat. She was shaking uncontrollably.

"Is it gone?" whispered Jean Marie.

"It's gone." Sandy roused herself and looked around. "But we still don't know where we are or how to get back."

"Perhaps at least we can row to the last place we turned and wait there," suggested Jean Marie.

"We can try, but as Dad warned, it may take a while to find us."

Again Jean Marie started to row back the way they had come. It was quite dark now. The trees which had provided pleasant shade in the day loomed up ominously before them. Except for the incessant croaking and twitterings of the night, all was silent. Raphaël didn't make a sound and Sandy, suddenly worried, tried to discern her still form in the dark.

"You okay back there?"

"I'm ... okay ... Sandy, you were very brave."

Brave! That was a laugh! "Listen, I'm sorry you two – I got you into this mess. I should have listened to Dad."

"It was a mistake, Sandy. You did not know we would get lost." Jean Marie answered. "Anyway," he laughed, "it's an adventure, an American adventure!"

"Thanks," said Sandy quietly. Suddenly she glanced up. "Did you see a light? There?" She pointed, her white arm barely visible. "Look, there it is again!"

"Yes, I see it!" Through the trees a light glittered in the distance.

"I think it's someone on the river, around the bend. I can hear a motor."

Soon, over the droning of the motor, they heard faint cries. Before long they could make them out. "Sandy! Jean Marie!"

"We're here!" Sandy called, "we're here!"

It seemed to take forever but after a time they could make out one boat, and then another.

"Is that you, Sandy?" She heard her uncle's voice.

"Yes, we're here!"

"Well, thank God!" She heard her father say as one of the boats pulled alongside, its bright lights blinding them.

"Are you all right?"

"We're fine, just a little hungry."

Sandy and Jean Marie helped Raphaël into the other boat. Then Jean Marie climbed in.

"You'd better get in Uncle Sam's boat," said her father.

"But what will we do with the row boat?"

"We'll tie it to the back here and bring it along."

When they were all settled and on their way back, Sandy yelled over the motor, "How did you find us?"

"Some fishermen spotted you and came with us to look for you. That's their boat your father's in. We've been searching a good three hours."

"I'm sorry," shouted Sandy.

Uncle Sam leaned closer, "The most important thing is that you're all right. We can't afford to lose any Bahá'ís at this point," he chuckled. "And maybe you've learned something."

"Yeah," Sandy said grimly. "Trying to be a good Bahá'í doesn't mean I'm a natural pathfinder!"

They said no more as Uncle Sam revved up the motor to catch up with the other boat.

When they finally made their way from the dock up to the cabin in pitch darkness, they all felt the effects of the nerve-racking day. They deposited their picnic basket and fishing equipment on the porch in a heap, too tired to put anything away.

"Well, you all just relax, I'm making dinner tonight," announced Sandy's father as he carried Jean Marie's fish into the kitchen.

"Raphaël, why don't you and Jean Marie get cleaned up. I'm too tired right now," said Sandy.

She flopped down on the couch. Uncle Sam, who had tagged along, sat in an armchair next to her.

"So, Snoopy," he asked with a twinkle in his eye, "How are your spiritual exercises coming along?"

"I've learned something, Uncle Sam."

"Oh, what?" he settled down more deeply into his chair.

"It's just that the whole key seems to be making yourself humble enough to admit your own faults — but at the same time keeping yourself confident enough that it's not the end of the world."

"Oh, my, that's a lot to learn in one day."

"What I mean is, that to see good qualities in other people you have to make room in your heart. And the only way to do that is to get rid of your own self-importance."

Uncle Sam studied Sandy a moment. "You know, it's taken me years of working on Local Spiritual Assemblies and committees to learn that. I mean, it's been in the writings all the time, but to understand it, one has to apply it.

"I remember a very difficult time I was passing through. We were having some rough moments on our LSA. There was a great deal of disunity. A lot of it stemmed from one member who in most outward respects was a good Bahá'í, but who had the most disturbing habit of criticizing everyone, including me. It's very hard to fight that. I have never been a good administrator and I am often negligent in fulfilling my duties. I forget, I procrastinate . . . Well, this was always being thrown in my face. And I was very defensive about it. I would boil with anger at every meeting, just waiting for one comment about my faults, and finding all sorts of ways that I would respond and put that person in their place. Well, at that time I was having a good many other severe tests, very severe tests. For one thing, I felt very alone after Aunt Mary's death.

"One night it seemed like the world was falling in and I broke down. I cried, I raged, I felt my heart would burst and . . . I prayed – harder than I ever had. In the deep stillness that followed, I lifted my head from my hands and suddenly it all came to me. First, that I was nothing, really nothing. That I would never be perfect, and that as long as I thought I was, I would be tormented. A deep acceptance settled in, an acceptance of my faults and a deep assurance of God's love, regardless. So what if I was negligent – I could work on it. The important thing was, to feel free to admit it to anyone who cared to know and to never feel defensive about it.

"At the next LSA meeting I practiced keeping this knowledge that I was nothing foremost in my mind. And I consciously tried to erase all negative thoughts, especially about this one person. And that, Sandy, was the beginning. Not the end, just the beginning, but it changed my life."

He paused, "You know, all those tests were like the watchman; they drove me up against the wall, until seeing no end, I leapt over it in desperation."

"Like in *The Seven Valleys*."

"You've been reading, Sandy," said Uncle Sam approvingly.

"Had to read it for deepening class."

"For me, at that time, the wall was my own sense of pride. I scaled it. But there are other walls. I only pray that God will give me enough tests to keep on scaling those walls."

"So, you pray for tests?"

"*'The food of them who haste to meet Thee is the fragments of their broken hearts.'*"

Sandy sat quietly for a long moment. Uncle Sam broke in gently, "So, it looks like God has given you a summer full of tests."

"Oh, I guess it's not that bad. I can try to teach."

"But you'll be teaching by your example."

"Oh, I don't know, Jean Marie seems a bit interested in the Faith."

"Hmmm ... You know we're having a talk this Saturday night on *The Promise of World Peace*. We might just invite them. Your father might even be interested."

"That's a great idea," Sandy said excitedly.

At that moment Jean Marie came into the room looking none the worse for the afternoon's adventure.

"Ah! I find you two alone together. I wonder, perhaps you would tell me more about this Bahá'í?

Uncle Sam and Sandy grinned at each other. "Perhaps we could," said Sandy, suppressing her smile, "if you're really interested."

ABOUT THE AUTHOR

After becoming a Bahá'í as a teenager, Susan Allen traveled as a pioneer to Taiwan and Togo before settling in the French-speaking African country, Gabon, eleven years ago. Susan is married with two daughters, Angela Marie and Elizabeth Marie, and a calico cat called Freckles.

Mail Order

MAIL ORDER

THE SECRET OF THE STOLEN MANDOLIN
Barbara Larkin

This exciting tale of exploration and intrigue follows the adventures of three children who answer a mysterious call for help and find themselves on a journey to another world. As the mystery unfolds, it soon becomes clear that this is no ordinary adventure, but a strange voyage of discovery!

A lively and entertaining narrative, true-to-life characters, and themes which explore prejudice, personal relationships and the purpose of life give this book enormous appeal for the 8-14 age group.

160pp softcover £2.25 / US$3.75

RIDE THE WAVE
Cindy Savage

Fame and fortune seem to come quickly to Riverview High School Bahá'í Club following the popularity of the first public performance of their 'Youth Wave' music/dance group, but will they be mature enough to cope with the consequences?

Written for the 10-16 age group, *Ride the Wave* explores the roller-coaster ride of adolescent life as Brandon, Tracey and their friends struggle to balance schoolwork, family, teaching and personal relationships. The first in a new series by this popular author.

96pp   softcover £3. 95 / US$6.95

THE PINCKELHOFFER MICE
Shirin Sabri

A charming allegorical tale of tremendous atmosphere and strength which reflects many of the problems faced by children in contemporary society. See how the Pinckelhoffer Mice cope with racism, sexism and class prejudice in this spirited adventure with a punch in its tail.

Bahá'í author Shirin Sabri's exciting narrative is perfectly complemented by beautiful illustrations by her mother, Sue Podger. Intended for the 8-14 age group.

160pp   illns.   softcover   £4.50 / US$7.95

BOOK REQUEST

Please write in block Capitals ✎

Name _____

Address _____

_____

_____

_____

Zip. _____ Date _____

Please send your order to:
Oneworld
Publications
185 Banbury Road
Oxford, OX2 7AR
England

Ph: (011-44) 865-310597
Fax: (011-44) 865-310598

Quantity	Title	Total
	The Pinckelhoffer Mice softcover US$ 7.95 / £4.50	
	The Stolen Mandolin softcover US$3.75 / £2.25	
	A For Effort softcover US$7.95 / £4.50	
	Nine Days to Istanbul softcover US$7.95 / £4.50	
	Ride the Wave softcover US$6.95 / 3.95	

Payment by:
____ Check/Money Order
____ American Express
____ Mastercard/Access
____ Diners Club
____ Visa
____ Bill Me

Sub Total ____
*Postage & Handling ____
Total ____

*Please add 15% to cover postage and handling (min. $2/£1)

Credit Card No. | | | | | | | | | | | | | | | | |

normally 16 digits

Exp. Date _____

Signature _____

Would your Community Librarian or friends like to receive details of these books? If so, just fill in their names and addresses below.

Name _____   Name _____

Address _____   Address _____

_____ Zip. _____   _____ Zip. _____